New Mexico Remembers 9/11

ISBN: 978-1-951122-10-2 (Paperback)
ISBN: 978-1-951122-15-7 (ebook)

LCCN: 2020936749
Copyright © 2020 by Patricia Walkow
Cover Design: Geoff Habiger

Printed in the United States of America.

Artemesia Publishing, LLC
9 Mockingbird Hill Rd
Tijeras, New Mexico 87059
www.apbooks.net
info@artemesiapublishing.com

New Mexico Remembers 9/11

Prose and Poetry by New Mexico Writers
Curated and Edited by Patricia Walkow

New Mexico in relation to the 9/11 attack sites. Attack locations from west to east: Shanksville, PA; Washington D.C. area; and New York City. Scenes from New Mexico.

The ability of the human spirit to surmount the tragedy of 9/11 is not forgotten in New Mexico.

—Elaine Carson Montague

Acknowledgements

A book of collective work requires the talent of its contributors, writers, and publisher. I would like to thank SouthWest Writers President, Rose Marie Kern, and New Mexico Press Women President, Sherri Burr for giving me the opportunity to present this project to their members. Their response was enthusiastic.

Thank you to the creators of prose and poetry. Your work graces these pages. Each author has a photograph and short biography at the end of this volume. Every time I read and reviewed their stories and poems, I had their faces before me and their voices in my mind. I now have more friends than when I embarked on this project, and hope to nurture those relationships in the future.

To my husband, Walter, thank you for many nights and days of enduring my physical presence, but mental absence as I prepared the manuscript for the publisher. You read each story and offered cogent suggestions. Thank you, Geoff Habiger of Artemesia Publishing for seeing the merit in these stories and for publishing *New Mexico Remembers 9/11*.

Patricia Walkow

We need to know we are something together which we are not and cannot be apart.

—Ryan P. Freeman

Contents

Poetry and Prose by Author

Author	Title
Joe Brown	*At Least I Could Do Something About It*
John J. Candelaria	*An Eyeful of Fear*
Pete Christensen	*Divide or Conquer?*
Teresa Civello	*The Home of the Brave*
Brenda Cole	*Comfort* *Subtle Changes*
Sylvia Ramos Cruz	*Where To?*
Mary E. Dorsey	*September*
Jesse Ehrenberg	*9/11*
Colin Patrick Ennen	*A Guilty Memory*
Roger Floyd	*The Sky*
Ryan P. Freeman	*That One September Day*
Cornelia Gamlem	*One Happy Island*
Paul D. Gonzales	*A Mourning in September*
Loretta Hall	*There's No Place Like Home*

Introduction

New Mexico Remembers 9/11 is the voice of New Mexico writers remembering the day Islamic extremists attacked the United States: September 1, 2001. Though two thousand miles from the target sites in New York, Washington, D.C., and in the skies above rolling fields in western Pennsylvania, New Mexicans were impacted. Neither cactus nor coyotes, lizards, roadrunners, or towering sage-studded mountains could emotionally separate them from people in our country who live "back east."

Although the writers whose work appears in this volume live in New Mexico now, at the time of the carnage, a few lived in New York, some in New Mexico, and others resided elsewhere. Yet, they drive home a common theme: no matter where you called "home" on that day, "home" was wherever one of the attacks occurred.

In evocative verse and prose, the authors recall an appalling day of brilliant blue autumn sky, crisp air, blood, confusion, anger, and death: What do I tell my children? How will I get home? What does this mean to my job? Why did this happen? What can I do?

When I decided to curate this collective work, I didn't realize 9/11 was still an actively-seeping wound requiring cauterization. Now, almost twenty years after the incident, people continue to grieve and try to make some sense of it.

Perhaps the writing helped.

Many expressed gratitude for the opportunity to be part of this work and it has been my honor to work with each contributor.

Patricia Walkow
October, 2020

The World Trade Center before the attack, after the attack, and the new Freedom Tower.

*The unmarred Pentagon, the building after the attack, and
a memorial bench for each life lost.*

A rock marks the spot in the field near Shanksville, Pennsylvania, where United Airlines Flight 93 crashed. The Tower of Voices and the visitor's center were erected in memoriam at the site.

I saw the sky, the sky that day,
That fateful day, that fateful day,
They came to die,
And so did I.

—*Roger Floyd*

The Sky

Roger Floyd

Dedicated to the memory of all who perished in the events of September 11, 2001.

I saw the sky, the azure sky,
So blue, I said, so blue, so high.
Beyond the sun, beyond the moon, beyond the sky,
They came, they ran, they came to die.
I ran, they ran, the time was nigh,
It came to me, the time to die.

The building held, the building fell,
I've come, I said, I've come to hell.
'Tis time to go, 'tis time to cry,
They came, they ran, they came to die.

Too high, I said, too high, too high!
I cannot see—they fly too high!
I cannot see! I cannot see!
I run, I run, I run to thee!
I saw a light, a light I said,
I saw a light, a firefly!
A firefly, so light, so high
I cannot see the firefly.
I felt the ground, too high, too high!
I cannot see! I cannot see!
I cannot see, I said,
I run, I run, I run to thee.
The sky was blue, so blue, that day,

And blue it stayed all day, all day,
And blue it stayed all day.
And night, it came, it came to me
As dark as night, no light I see.
No sky, no light, no light I see,
No light for me to find the sky,
The sky, the sky, the azure sky.
I'm damned to be the one who saw,
Who saw the sky, the sky above, the azure sky.

I wondered why, I wonder why,
From A to Z, to go and buy,
To let them go, to tell them no,
To tell them yes—Oh, no! Oh, no!
I told them no, but no, they came,
They came to see, to see the sky, the azure sky.
To see the sky they flew so high,
So high, so high, though night be nigh,
I saw the sky, the azure sky.

The building high, the building low,
The ground above, the ground below,
Upon the Earth the building lay,
The sky, it seems, was blue that day.
But blue it seems was not the kind
That came to me and rent my mind
And took from me the one I love
From ground below and sky above.
I saw the sky, the sky that day,
That fateful day, that fateful day,
They came to die,
And so did I.

It came to me, I now know why!
I now know why I saw the sky!
But no, I said, but no, I lie,
The causes deep that underlie
I cannot tell, I don't know why.
I don't know why I saw the sky.

On homeward bound, with letters bound,
With time to think, with time to sigh,
I cannot tell, I cannot tell,
I don't know why I saw the sky.
Of all the things I saw that day,
The only thing I know so high,
I know not why I saw the sky.
I'll tell you though, the sky, the sky,
It may be high, that azure sky,
It may be high, so high, so high,
But let the world not yet forget,
Not yet forget the sky, the sky,
The sky above, the azure sky.

Tonight, tomorrow, by and by,
The time will come for you and I,
The time will come to say goodbye,
I'll see you there above the sky.
But till that time, when time has come,
There comes a time when you and I
Must go and come and fly so high,
So high, so high, above the sky.

But till that time, no sky, no dark,
No raven's call, no lupine bark,
Can take from me, can take from thee
The time we spent in joyful glee
Beyond the sky, beyond the sea.
Yea, verily,
Will we forget? Forget the sky?
Oh, no, I said, oh, no, not I.

What About our Children?

It took great effort then to be brave, but I had to for my children.

—Carolyn Kuehn

This is the child I prayed for and begged for. This is the child I thought I would never have...

"Momma...I can't reveal where we are going...this is what I trained for," he replied, sounding like a grown man.

—*Marilyn L. Pettes Hill*

A Mother's Heart

Marilyn L. Pettes Hill

My bucket list of places to visit included Portland, Oregon. Even though I was going there for a tax conference with two coworkers and my boss, I was thrilled about the trip.

The September 10, 2001 flight was smooth and uneventful. The evening was spent sightseeing and walking along the beautiful tree-lined streets. Seeing the statue of Portlandia, trident in hand, weighing in at a mighty six-and-a-half short tons was a highlight of the walk. After returning to our hotel later in the evening, preparations were made for our conference scheduled for the next morning—September 11.

As I was getting dressed for the first day of the conference, I received a phone call from my only biological child. He was home in Albuquerque visiting and recruiting after going through basic training in Ft. Benning, Georgia and Advanced Individual Training (AIT) at Ft. Huachuca, Arizona. I picked up the phone and heard his frantic voice, thinking something bad had happened at home.

"Momma, do you have the TV on?" he asked.

"No." I replied, "I'm getting ready to go downstairs

for my conference." I quickly turned on the TV and watched the images in horror.

"Oh my God!" was all I could say as I flopped down on the bed in shock.

We talked for a while, discussing what we were seeing and we learned that it could be a terrorist attack. That was just the first tower. But it wasn't over! It was just the beginning.

"I've got to get downstairs for my conference. I will call you later. Love you!" I exclaimed as I ended the call.

When I arrived at the ballroom for the opening session, most of my colleagues were standing in the hall looking at the TV. I thought everyone looked shocked. There was an eerie silence and solemn atmosphere as people began to grasp the gravity of the situation.

One of the IRS attendees said, "Oh my God! We have staff in that tower!"

As the morning went on, many attendees mentioned they knew people in the towers and the Pentagon. I did not personally know anyone, but my heart was broken, and I suspected the hearts of millions of Americans were broken.

At that point, what I most wanted was to be with my family—to hug and kiss them and thank God for their safety.

But I didn't know at the time that this tragedy would indeed affect my family in a very personal way.

The conference became secondary and almost trivial at that point. People made calls to family and friends and then to airlines to try to get flights home, but all air traffic in the U.S. was halted.

We had a serious dilemma. How would we get home? One of my co-workers rented the car for us before we arrived in Portland. She decided to call the rental car company to arrange its return.

"Oh, no you don't!" I exclaimed. "What if the airlines are not back in the air for *days*?"

I told her to call the car rental company and tell them we wanted to drive the car to Albuquerque. I didn't care about the drop-off fee. She called and to our amazement, the representative said the fee would be waived. This was the first of many amazingly kind moments that I experienced as a result of 9/11.

The following day we began our approximately 1,386-mile unexpected drive from Portland, Oregon to Albuquerque, New Mexico. I was grateful we had a car, because at this point, there were few, if any, rental cars available. I heard people were *buying* cars in order to get home. Thankfully, we did not have to drive to the east coast, as did many of my colleagues.

I had never driven through the Pacific northwest. Although it was a tragic time, I tried to make the best of a bad situation. Seeing all the beauty and nature around me, I thought that life is beautiful. America is beautiful.

My coworkers and I had worked together well, but traveling 1,386 miles in a car should have been awkward, at best. We talked about family and work and the scenery around us. We even joked. Humor was imperative in these troubled times. We discussed the events that transpired and how we thought they would change America. Of course, we had no clue about the magnitude of the changes to come.

We spent the night about halfway between Portland and Albuquerque and met the nicest people along the way. Perfect strangers talked to each other with kindness and concern. I'm not sure if they were nice before 9/11, but I'd like to think they were. Some fishermen at the hotel had been on the coast and planned to fly back home. Instead, they bought a large cooler to transport their fresh fish home by rental car.

——∿∾∿——

I had never been so happy to arrive home. It seemed like I had been gone for years. Although I felt safe in my sanctuary, I knew that might not be true in the coming months. Yet, it didn't seem to matter where you were or what you were doing, you might not ever be safe again.

When I was young, I remember my mom telling me not to go to certain places and with certain people. The general consensus was that if I followed these guidelines, I would be safe.

After 9/11, everything everywhere was different.

People were nicer, more patient and kind. Almost everyone in America expressed pride in being an American or living in America. Flags flew on buildings and cars and were imprinted on T-shirts, socks, even underwear.

But the down side was the atmosphere of prevailing fear. What did this tragedy mean? We thought, as Americans, no one would have the audacity to commit such a heinous crime against our country. After all, we were a superpower. And so, our belief was shattered.

On one hand we were kinder and gentler. On the other hand, anyone who slightly resembled the terrorists were shunned and eyed with suspicion and distrust.

~ level ~

Although my son was in Albuquerque on 9/11, he was scheduled to report to the 82nd Airborne Division at Ft. Bragg, North Carolina at the end of the month. I said my tearful goodbyes (I always cry when we separate), and he reported for duty. When he arrived at Ft. Bragg, the authorities told him not to get too comfortable because they were getting ready to leave for training. They went to a remote location in California. Soon thereafter, I was sent to California for a work meeting. I was happy that I could visit him. We went to Disneyland—again.

In the spring of 2002, he called to tell me his division was going overseas.

"What?" I screamed. "Where are you going?"

He sighed and said "I can't tell you, Momma."

"What do you mean you can't tell me?" I raised my voice in reply.

"Momma, I'm Military Intelligence so I can't reveal where we are going," he replied like a soldier.

"I'm going to call the Governor! You're my *only* son. Don't they have a law that only-sons don't have to go to war?" I asked emphatically.

"No Momma, that's no longer valid. And I want to go. This is what I trained for," he replied, sounding like a grown man.

Oh. My. God. They have brain-washed him already.

"We're shipping out in July."

"Well, I want to come to see you before you go," I said in resignation. My heart sank as I fought the brimming tears.

—ᴓᴓᴓ—

I flew to Raleigh, North Carolina and he picked me up at the airport. I hugged him so tightly I thought I would squeeze the life out of him. We talked as we drove to Ft. Bragg. He still would not tell me where he was going and he talked in generalities. When we arrived at my hotel, the young registration clerk asked me where I was from.

"Albuquerque, New Mexico," I replied.

"Really?" he exclaimed in shock. "I thought 'I knew I shoulda taken a left turn at Albuquerque,' was only a Bugs Bunny cartoon thing."

"It's a real place" I replied.

He asked what I was doing at Ft. Bragg and I told him my son was getting ready to ship out.

He said, "Oh yeah, the 82nd is deploying to Afghanistan."

I turned and looked at my son with incredulity. He just shrugged nonchalantly. When we took my luggage to my room I asked, "How is it that the hotel registration clerk knows where you are going?"

He shrugged again and said, "The people around Fayetteville and Ft. Bragg seem to know everything that happens on base."

So much for military intelligence. But I was grateful for

this almost all-knowing registration clerk.

Of course, this knowledge brought up a plethora of additional questions. My momma always said I was a nosy child. Well, there is certainly a time and place for over-the-top curiosity. I wanted to know where in Afghanistan and how long, and, and, and, and....

Being who he is, my son just said, "Momma, you know I can't tell you."

Leaving Ft. Bragg was one of the hardest things I had ever done. My only child was going to war!

This is the child I prayed for and begged God for. This is the child I thought I would never have. I went through a multitude of fertility pills, tests and procedures. I took my temperature to gauge when would be the best time to conceive. I spent years and money trying to conceive. Finally, I gave up on testing and worrying. It was just too heartbreaking every month to learn I was not pregnant.

My son called me when he arrived safely somewhere in the Middle East. AFGHANISTAN!

"Hi, Momma."

"Hello, son!" How are you?" I asked with concern.

"I'm fine. I can't stay on the phone long and I don't know how often I will be able to call you since I will be in the field most of the time. We come into base periodically, but there are only a few phones for all the troops."

"Call me whenever you can, day or night, it doesn't matter. I love you son, and please be careful."

"Love you too, Momma."

From that moment on, I had my cell phone practically taped to my hip. I informed my boss, co-workers, and staff that if my son called, I would stop whatever I was doing to accept his call. The calls helped calm me. They assured me he was alright—or at least alive.

He told me that I could send items to him and said to send a lot of everything because they shared and some soldiers did not get anything from home. Enough said. I sent as much jerky, cookies, nuts, baby wipes, and foot powder that I could to the infamous APO—the "Army Post Office." The APO lets you send mail and packages to Army or Air Force personnel—regardless of where they are in the world—but charges you only standard domestic rates.

I watched news networks every non-working, non-sleeping minute. My sister in Texas was doing the same. During my numerous online searches, I learned that there was a newspaper in Fayetteville, North Carolina. Their news folks seemed to know almost everything! I would often log on to see what was happening with the 82nd. The paper also took pictures and interviewed overseas troops on a regular basis. I scrolled through the news and pictures like a madwoman. I never saw my son.

After six long months, my son told me he was coming home; I was ecstatic. I told him that I wanted to see his eyes. What I did not say was that I wanted to make sure he was *really* OK. I was in the meat and fish aisle in Walmart when he called to tell me his plane touched down in the United States. I shouted and jumped up and down. The people around probably thought I was insane, but I didn't care. There was nothing but pure joy…happiness…thankfulness.

War is its own kind of hell. Some people cannot truly understand what our children, our friends, our colleagues, our first responders—and our soldiers, go through to protect our freedom and how 9/11 affected so many lives. I am grateful to those who lost their lives in *all* wars and I pray God's peace for the remaining family members and friends of 9/11's victims.

And I am forever grateful and thankful that my son—*my heart*—is still here.

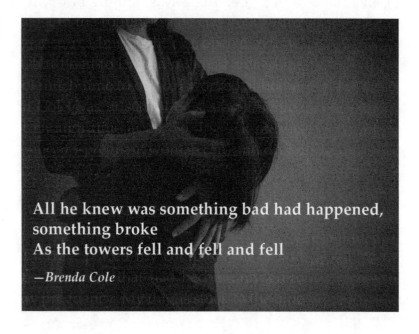

All he knew was something bad had happened,
something broke
As the towers fell and fell and fell

—*Brenda Cole*

Comfort

Brenda Cole

Cooking breakfast for my first grader, juggling the
morning schedule in my head
Son to school, me to teach
Then the phone call
Strained, urgent
"Turn on the TV"
I reached for the set in the kitchen
And a plane crashing into a skyscraper erupted onto
the screen
I stared mesmerized, horrified
as the same shot repeated again and again and again
and then the soft, warm little body
against my left side
then the towers fell
the roar, clouds, screams
and the sudden terrified arms digging a hole in my
side
I turned my body, shut off the stove, TV
And gathered the stiff, frozen child to me.
We curled on the couch, my body and the afghan
shielding his trembling form
All he knew was something bad had happened, something broke

As the towers fell and fell and fell
My seven-year-old son burrowed into my chest search-
ing for his own stability
I wove a net around him of Legos, silly movies, and a
day off school.
And in my mind the towers fell and fell and fell
And the world as my son and I knew it, changed.

You know, this is the first time since we came to America that I do not feel safe.

—Walter Walkow, as mentioned to him by Ella Walkow

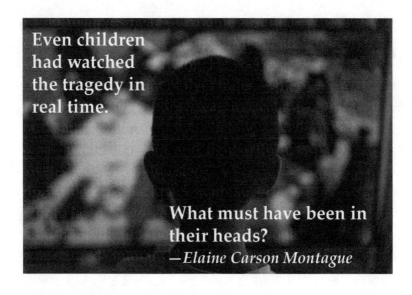

Even children
had watched
the tragedy in
real time.

What must have been in
their heads?
—*Elaine Carson Montague*

Even the Children Watched

Elaine Carson Montague

The shower felt good, gently massaging taut shoulder muscles and my back. School had been in session for about a month, and I was accustomed to our morning routine. As I finished drying off with a large, plush motel towel, I looked forward to relaxing in the small dressing area where I could use well-lit mirrors to apply makeup and fix my hair.

But I heard, "Honey, come in here now!" leaving no doubt about the urgency in the plea from the area that was living room, bedroom, and kitchen.

My husband, Gary, sat on the short sofa and pointed at the television. He was excited and telling me something, but so was the broadcaster. I knew right away the smoking building was part of the World Trade Center. Would Godzilla rise above the scene in this horror movie? I stood glued to the spot in the bathroom doorway, stared at the unbelievable but real bodies falling and the black clouds of ugly smoke, and tried to make sense of what Gary and the commentator said while my mind denied it.

This was a hard time for us because my dad had died in July, only seven weeks earlier. When we returned to Albuquerque from Silver City, we inhaled a foul odor

21

and found our hardwood floors destroyed by 17,000 gallons of water which had escaped from a faulty toilet. That led to mold in the crawlspace, which resulted in strangers boxing almost every item and scrap of our lives and placing them in climate-controlled storage miles from our home. We ourselves were stored at a local inn in a living space slightly smaller than my 600 square-foot portable classroom at a nearby elementary school. Teaching materials, the check ledger, address book, and necessities filled the car trunk. Gary, retired and unable to drive, was captive to the suite.

The broadcaster kept repeating the story—an airplane hit the tower—over and over as the scene replayed. He sounded in shock. Abruptly, before my transfixed eyes, another plane flew into the South Tower.

"No, no, no!" I was yelling. Gary was yelling.

Looping replays showed the first tower smoking and crumbling and human beings falling to the ground.

Horrified, we hugged each other and wiped away tears of shock and sadness as reality shook our beings. We prayed for mercy and compassion. I hurried to school to arrive ahead of the children and learned the Pentagon had been hit. Was my friend Brenda inside that five-sided building for the meeting she was scheduled to attend? What plane had she taken?

TVs were on in the school office and every classroom as I went through otherwise silent halls. Stillness settled over small clusters of colleagues watching together, seeking support. We searched each other's faces without a word. America was under attack. Where was the President? What happened? Who dared do this? The principal urged us to proceed as normal, not to have the TVs on during class, and to discuss what happened only if the students brought it up, especially in the lower grades. During the day, details reached me, but I don't remember how: all planes were grounded, the South Tower fell, another plane crashed in Pennsylvania. Was it headed to the White House? President Bush declared the 9/11 attack a terrorist act. The North Tower collapsed.

Those buildings were tall and held a lot of ordinary people like us. How many were hurt or killed? When would this stop? Gary and I comforted each other through quick cell calls whenever my student groups changed. He felt defeated that he could not do anything to help the situation, depressed that it happened in the United States, that our country was being torn down by people who hated us. He thought of uncles who fought in World War II and the favorite one who died, and wondered if this would draw us into another global war. How would this day affect prices of ordinary things, such as food, clothing, and gasoline? How would it change our lives? He remembered rationing and shortages. Gary felt sad for families of those lost that day and tried to distract himself by working on the computer. He felt lonelier than usual while I was gone for eight hours. The motel was not where he wanted to be, with his tools and the comforts of home inaccessible.

I also do not recall when my teaching partner, who was Muslim, realized how strongly people would generalize their fears and anger into hatred of people of her religion as a result of the attack or what she and her professor husband endured. When Waco occurred, we had talked about the Taliban. She said it was a radical group which did not represent all Muslims any more than David Koresh and the Branch Davidians at Waco or Jim Jones of the Peoples Temple cult in Jonestown, Guyana, represented all Christians.

But vivid is the face of a bright seven-year-old girl who looked up into my eyes with her forehead wrinkled. She always had that same big wrinkle between her brows when she did not understand something or faced unfairness.

"Mrs. Montague, did you hear about the terrible accident this morning?" she asked.

Throughout the day, several groups of children ages seven to eleven cycled through my class because they tested high in intelligence and needed challenges beyond the regular curriculum. Some were far ahead of their peers academically, while a handful lagged. They brought an abundance of creativity. Critical thinking took their minds to places beyond their years.

"It wasn't an accident, Sara," I spoke and held her, hoping to be a voice of reason and reassurance. "We don't know who did it or why. We'll find out."

Even children had watched the tragedy in real time. My mind had trouble translating what I saw into language I could begin to understand. What must have been in their heads? The questions, discussions, worries and opinions of that day escape memory. The Pledge of Allegiance took on special significance. The words of the National Anthem ran through my mind and challenged me to understand at a deeper level than I had ever needed to before. Perilous fight with bombs bursting. Had war come to our soil? Who was the enemy? The day made me think of President Kennedy's assassination and how I watched the flag above the post office. If it flew at full mast, I knew he was alive. Then it was lowered.

In the afternoon of 9/11, yet another building in the complex—Seven World Trade Center—fell.

Patriotism surged in New Mexico and across the United States in the following days. One chain sold almost half a million flags nationwide on September 11, 12, and 13. The oldest American flag-making company, Annin, quadrupled its production but had trouble matching demand. American flags flew from vehicles, in yards, and on little girls' hair ribbons, and men wore flag pins in their lapels and on their ties. I thought of the wooden flagpole which was used to display the colors every day from my father's deck and how it was probably leaning against the same inside wall as it was after his funeral.

I found favorite places to listen to church bells tolling. Like most of the nation, we prayed publicly and privately and sang patriotic songs, rejoicing at tales of heroes. We attended commemorations for those lost. After a large Prayer for America service, most Americans talked about an operatic New York policeman who sang "God Bless America." In the days after that, he inspired us with "The Star-Spangled Banner" and "Amazing Grace" and continued to work at Ground Zero, as the area of destruction in New York City was called. This was a time we believed most citizens mourned individually and united with others as one. We stopped what we were doing, stayed closer to home, thought about our lives and families, and tried to consider different perspectives as we sought to better our attitudes. Like a wave that calms, however, huge flag purchases were temporary and subsided. So, sadly, were widespread introspection, donating to charity, and blood donations.

One evening, as Gary and I ate Mexican food in the cantina at Casa de Benavidez with its waterfalls, ponds, and plantings, a TV fundraiser concert for victims and first responders played in the background. Not long after, I bought a tee-shirt at the Owl Café displaying a color image of the towers emblazoned with "Never Forget 9-11." I wear it every year on the September anniversary in honor of the 6,000 people who were hurt and the almost 3,000 people we lost, including 200 who fell from the towers. I learned my friend had not gone to the Pentagon as scheduled, but it still felt like a personal violation. We wondered how many people might suffer lasting nightmares and lung damage or be haunted by images from the disaster.

My days were long. Three times a week, the seven-hour workday stretched another couple of hours for water exercise and errands. We had asked the post office to forward our mail to the motel while mold abatement and restoration continued at home. I worried when we had no mail. One evening, Gary said the afternoon management told him FedEx was holding a package I sent.

"What package? I didn't send a package by FedEx," I said.

It took quite a bit of tracking the mystery package

and a phone call to learn that the woman working at the inn's front desk each morning had bundled six weeks of our mail instead of giving it to us. We lived directly outside of the dining area of the main building, where she saw us daily. I inquired in the afternoons, and that clerk always reported we had no mail. That was because the morning clerk had mailed the bundle to our home by FedEx on 9/11. The government, however, had grounded all planes on 9/11, including FedEx. The package, caught in a loop, made its way back to the inn. The morning clerk returned it to FedEx. Fortunately, the afternoon clerk received a call from FedEx saying a package was being held for us.

My personal struggle about whether to retire increased as house repairs dragged on. In my thirty-first year, I loved teaching. The children delighted me with their laughter and insight. I missed sharing their cute sayings with my father in our weekly telephone conversations. Each morning seemed harder to leave Gary at the inn. I don't know how much might be attributed to 9/11, but combining national tension with the house and feeling like I was living out of the back of our car took its toll. Late one afternoon, the trunk refused to close. The representative at the dealership said he would stay open late and fix it, so we made a fast trip across town. It was in the last days of October when I told my husband I had something serious to discuss.

"You want to retire, don't you?" he asked. "Not now.

You will go stark raving mad in this place. Wait till we are back in the house."

Every month, the insurance man said, "Thirty days. We'll be done in thirty days."

Despite disappointments of delays, we could not complain without feeling guilty and knew our problems were no way close to the trauma so many felt after 9/11.

In December, I needed a warm coat for playground duty. We bought winter clothes because ours were in storage. We shopped for a Christmas tree and ornaments, decorated our room, and hung large, colorful stockings. We also decided to leave the megachurch we had attended for eight years. After the holiday, we returned to our old church to renew relationships and nourish our strong faith in a more intimate community.

The 9/11 attacks were preceded and followed by other terrorist behaviors and wars in Iraq, Afghanistan, and Pakistan. Nineteen hijackers from several countries perpetrated the Twin Towers assault, all members of al Qaeda. Most were from Saudi Arabia. Four came from the United Arab Emirates, Egypt, and Lebanon. Some of the pilots had flight training in the United States. The War on Terror was launched, and a mastermind was identified. We asked ourselves if we and our government had paid attention.

We moved home seven-and-a-half months later, in March. I retired at the end of the school year.

Discord and oppression in the Middle East extend to this day. The children who watched smoking towers and saw real people falling to their deaths saw a reality I never wanted them to see. Did that make them feel less secure, more stressed and vulnerable? The young ones I taught have never experienced national peace as I once did. Conspiracy theories persist about 9/11, embroiling Americans in controversy.

There are no easy answers, and not all actions achieve satisfactory solutions. Some people hurry through life, helping them avoid any thought of what happened almost twenty years ago; however, we have reminders. The New York wreckage of the Twin Towers was replaced with a memorial, and an Albuquerque church has two of the steel beams pulled from the ash to represent rebirth through fortitude and faith. My Muslim friend moved away, but she and I correspond and continue to pray for each other. And the children grew up, many seeking to build a more caring world through personal achievement and political action.

The ability of the human spirit to surmount the tragedy of 9/11 is not forgotten in New Mexico

..."What are you doing?"
..."Just playing."
He zoomed a toy airplane through the air.

..."Crrrrr...ashhh." The plane toppled the Lego tower, scattering pieces everywhere.

- *Carolyn Kuehn*

That Day

Carolyn Kuehn

As I sat in my minivan waiting for Cole and his Montessori teacher, I smiled at the day: the sun's unwavering warmth, leaves still clinging to their branches, creating a tapestry of orange, yellow, and red against a clear sky. It was the kind of day that made people happy.

Within minutes, there he was, heading back to my car, squeezing his teacher's hand with his little one, eyes red with tears already flowing and those preparing to.

"Mommy come back, Mommy come back," he cried, repeating a verse from his favorite music video. Releasing himself from her grip, he ran across the parking lot and to the car.

"Thank you, Mrs. P, we'll be back in a minute." Cole climbed into the passenger seat and I curled my arms around his tiny two-year-old body as best I could, a difficult task given that I was nine-months pregnant.

"Mommy come back," he repeated.

"Mommy *always* comes back, Sweetie." I kissed the top of his head, inhaling his smell of waffles and maple syrup, of a sweet breakfast, of a precious toddler.

We stopped the tears and trudged back to the door of his classroom. I'm sure we looked like Winnie the Pooh and Piglet walking together on that memorable blustery day. Big and little, bonded together, holding hands.

After weeks of non-stop crying when going into school, Cole was now able to tolerate all but the first few minutes without me. So, I stood in the corner while he began to adjust to the routine of the classroom — the Pledge of Allegiance, reading on the rug, open playtime.

It was hard, but I had to leave him. I had a deadline to meet and not much time to do so. I worked at home, but only when Cole was at school or sleeping, which was really not enough time at all. So, I snuck out (as much as a nine-month-pregnant woman can) and drove home.

I set up a TV tray, placed my computer on it, and nestled into the Lazy Boy that had become my go-to chair during my pregnancy. My thighs stuck to the blue leather, sweat pooled behind my knees.

Within minutes, the phone rang. *Already interrupted.* My first impulse was to ignore the call. Instead, I flipped open my cell phone. "Hello?"

"Turn on the TV now." Peter's voice had unusual force.

"Why?" I was in the middle of writing a report for a client.

"Just do it." This was strange. We rarely watched television during the work week, unless it was sports.

The remote lay across the room. I put one hand on each side of my body and pushed myself up, belly first, and turned it on.

"Oh my God," I gasped. The first tower burning. The newscasters were calling it a freak accident. The second plane hit. Another hit the Pentagon. Now they were calling it a terrorist attack, an act of war. And then news of yet another hijacking—United Flight 93—where passengers fought back, crashing the plane into a field in Shanksville, Pennsylvania, instead of its suspected target: the White House.

"Come home. Please come home." I did not want to be alone with this. Nausea lodged in my stomach; my skin became clammy. I leaned my head back on the seat, closed my eyes, and took deep breaths to quell the shock.

Peter and I both knew how lucky we were. He was supposed to be one hundred miles away from Philadelphia—our home—at Two World Financial Center, a building across the street from the World Trade Center; but his meeting had been rescheduled for Friday.

What if the meeting hadn't been changed? What if he had been walking outside? What if he had been eating lunch at Windows on the World? What-ifs clogged my mind.

Once home, Peter called his colleagues there. They were safe so far, but at close range, they could see the people leaping, one after another, from the towers. What were they thinking? What kind of choices did they have? Burning to death, suffocating, or dying by jumping from one hundred stories?

Focused on the televised evacuation efforts, we witnessed the ultimate horror—the crumbling towers, releasing clouds of smoke and ash that sprinted down the streets, chasing survivors and unsuspecting pedestrians.

Whereas many were reminded of Pearl Harbor, watching the airplanes ripping through the towers reminded me of my dad's story from World War II, when kamikazes attacked the aircraft carrier USS Saratoga, a scene that he witnessed firsthand. It was a story he repeated his whole life. Even as dementia clouded his mind, it was the one memory he never forgot.

Our first instinct was to get Cole. Cars crowded the parking lot. Almost every other parent had the same idea. It was as if we all wanted to cocoon in our own homes, with just our families, in seemingly safe havens.

Once home, I picked up Cole and took him upstairs, away from the television, away from those unimaginable scenes. In his room, we rocked in the rocking chair, our routine before his afternoon nap. I tried to sing his favorite song, but the words just wouldn't come.

"What's wrong, Mommy?" At two-years-old, Cole was in tune with my emotions, seeing and sensing my fear.

"Something bad just happened." My lips trembled as my eyes glossed over with imminent tears.

"To us?" As he studied my face, his own revealed alarm that this *something* had hurt our family's little world.

"No. Don't worry, Sweetie. Everything is fine."

Was it?

"We're okay," I added.

But were we?

How could I answer his questions, when I, as the supposedly all-knowing parent, couldn't even answer them myself?

This was not the kind of world we had envisioned for Cole and his soon-to-be sister. Previously exciting things, like buying a clown mobile and tiny pink moccasins, painting the nursery a cheery yellow, and putting rose-covered sheets on the crib mattress, became frivolous, even trivial, in comparison to this disaster.

The joy of anticipating a new baby and preparing for its arrival had been stolen from us.

I was captivated by the endless loop of horrific images, unable to stop watching, reading, and listening. I wanted to believe that somehow it never happened, that it was all an illusion, a nightmare, some kind of bad mistake.

The news media catered to my needs, with nonstop coverage of the attacks, their aftermath, details of the day, bystanders' accounts, acts of heroism on United Flight 93 and in the towers, profiles of the victims. I watched late into the night, after Cole and Peter had gone to bed. I craved information, the good and the bad. It was as if by knowing, I could be prepared for the next attack, that by worrying I could somehow prevent it.

"Cole, what are you doing?" Sounds of smashing toys reached the kitchen where I was making chocolate chip cookies, trying to restore some normalcy to our lives in those first few days after the attacks. I wiped my doughy hands on my apron and moved into the adjacent family room.

"Just playing." He zoomed a toy airplane through the air.

Since we had no relatives near our home in Philadelphia, we frequently flew to see them in Michigan, Florida, and Las Vegas. Cole loved flying. He was a seasoned traveler, with as many frequent flyer miles as me: a little boy who cherished the window seat, marveling at the fluffy clouds and miniature towns below, a boy who, in later years, would bargain and fight with his sister for that coveted view from the sky.

For every trip, I filled his backpack with surprises, little things meant to keep a two-year-old engaged and happy for a multi-hour flight: stickers, new crayons, coloring books, a stuffed animal, Play-Doh®, bubblegum. But what occupied him most did not come in the backpack. It was always the small airplane replica we purchased from the airport souvenir shop moments before departure. Each airplane was slightly different and even had real names: American, United, Delta. With all our trips, he had acquired quite a collection.

"Crrrrr...ashhh." The plane toppled the Lego tower, scattering pieces everywhere.

We had not been careful. We were not censoring our discussions or curtailing our listening to NPR during the day or the nightly news at dinner.

We changed. We had to. We read newspaper accounts silently and only watched television after Cole was sound asleep, no longer asking for water or one more hug, but with mouth gaping open, tiny breaths barely audible.

─☙☙─

My mother-in-law wanted to be here for the birth. She lived in Las Vegas, Nevada, a six-hour plane ride to Philadelphia.

"You don't need to come, Mom." Peter and I were worried, not sure if it was safe to fly. All planes had been grounded in the days after 9/11; flights were only starting up again, and airport security...well...we didn't trust it.

She—a tiny, five-foot-two dynamo—was determined to come and could not be deterred. "No terrorist can stop me from seeing my new granddaughter."

And so, she came. Alone. In an empty plane.

Exactly two weeks after the attacks, on Tuesday, September 25th, 2001, I gave birth to our daughter Lydia, a healthy, beautiful six-pound, two-ounce baby.

The birth was uneventful. The nurses were quiet and respectful. The halls were silent. We asked, "What was it like that day?" Everyone knew what that day was. "Quiet, like today," was all they said.

My fears worsened after the attack. Public places closed indefinitely: Independence Hall, the Liberty Bell, all national monuments. I was afraid to make previously simple and thoughtless excursions to the Acme supermarket, the King of Prussia mall, the local Barnes & Noble, any place where more than a few people gathered.

Whereas some reacted with anger, rage even, I could not get past the sadness and feelings of helplessness. It took just one September morning to shatter my sense of security, even though, in reality, we had never really been safe. We knew that America-haters abounded, but even so, we were unable to conceive the depth of that hatred until those fuel-laden missiles disintegrated our symbols of wealth and power. We had been caught off-guard, and life would never be the same.

I hugged Cole tighter, I held Lydia longer, and said "I love you" many more times each day. I treasured the precious distractions that my little ones provided at that time and in the days that followed. Cole: making "soup-salad" from mud and weeds, searching for caterpillars and inch worms, sleeping with a plastic backhoe, conversing with space aliens. Lydia: sharing toothless grins, grabbing my glasses off with her chubby fingers, crawling to her brother, pointing at her first rainbow.

It took great effort then to be brave, but I had to for my children. I had to be strong for them and believe for them that this world would not be forever dangerous and defined by evil, but that good would come once again.

Mommy come back.

We have a box in the garage with 9/11 "memorabilia" — special editions of *Time* and *Newsweek*, yellowing newspapers with headlines such as "U.S. Attacked," and "Day of Infamy." We thought that one day our children would want to know what it was like, what happened that day, why everyone makes such a big deal about it.

When Lydia and Cole were in middle school, we watched documentaries together, read firsthand accounts, and answered their questions. Sporadically, depending on the teacher, they participated in a moment of silence on the anniversary of the attacks; but they didn't spend much time, if any, discussing it in their classes.

For us, though, for our generation, it was a day we would never forget, the day our nation experienced evil firsthand, when our innocence was pulverized, just like the towers. It was the end of a simple life of being good, doing good, and having everything turn out okay.

Yet, in an odd way, the attacks were a respite for our nation and our world: a hiatus from partisan politics, boundaries and borders, international disputes. At least for a short time anyway. American flags unearthed or purchased began appearing everywhere, in other countries even. France's newspaper *Le Monde* declared, "We are all Americans."

It was a time when the world came together in prayer, connected as humans, exhibiting acts of compassion and self-sacrifice, international hospitality. I believe that clinging to this universal benevolence was the only way we were able to cope with the terror—to focus not on the danger of strangers, but on their kindness instead.

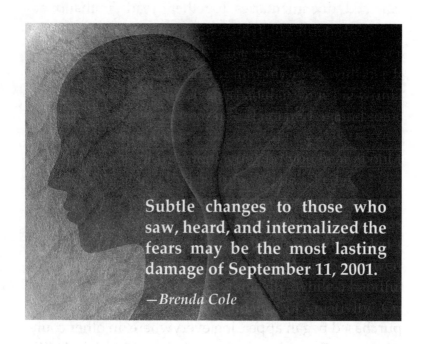

Subtle changes to those who saw, heard, and internalized the fears may be the most lasting damage of September 11, 2001.

—*Brenda Cole*

Subtle Changes

Brenda Cole

Nothing quite compares with being a single parent. Take all the issues and worries that are split between two parents living in the same house and magnify them a thousand-fold for each of you when you live in separate houses.

My ex-husband and I had been lucky. When we divorced, we were each grown-up enough to put our son's well-being first. So aside from Dan still complaining about his dad and I having two different houses, he seemed to be adapting well. He was a well-adjusted, happy, adorable six-year-old.

The morning of 11 September 2001 subtly changed my son's world forever.

Dan lived with me and spent time each week at his dad's house. His biggest concerns until that morning were: how many movies would he be able to watch, how soon would he be able to play with his best friend, Ali, and don't let the cats steal the Legos.

Then, on that fateful day, I was in the kitchen making breakfast. I was about to try and get my son out of bed for the third time when the phone rang. Before I even got out a complete hello, my ex hoarsely demanded that I turn on the TV. He was on a business trip to Portland, Oregon and I was concerned because he sounded scared, not a usual tone for him. I flipped on the small set in the kitchen and thought I'd caught a disaster movie. What was with the plane crashing into the skyscraper? Just about then, I felt a pair of arms curl about my waist and a sleepy head lean into my left side. I turned off the stove, gave Dan a quick hug and tried to get some sense out of his father. I turned back to the TV and again saw the same shot of the plane crashing into the building. Reality still hadn't dawned on me. Then a second plane hit the other tower. I suddenly realized this was the World Trade Center in New York and worse, this just might not be a movie.

My ex was trying to tell me something about multiple plane strikes in New York. My son was still leaning half asleep against my hip, and I was trying to comprehend the seemingly impossible when I heard the screaming. I looked up and saw the tower crumbling. Massive clouds of ash and concrete—looking for all the world like a pyroclastic cloud from a volcano—poured down over the running, screaming hordes of people.

The body leaning against me trembled, his hands clutching at my waist. Turning, I blocked the TV with my body until I could turn it off and quickly led my son to the couch and onto my lap. All he knew was something bad had happened. I knew little more than the location. My mind was still trying to deny what was trying to become reality. This was the United States; tornados, hurricanes…sure, but multiple planes flying into skyscrapers? No way.

As I held my trembling child, I realized I still had no idea what was going on. Grabbing the phone, I called his dad. Wrapped in an afghan, we waited for my ex to pick up the phone. When he came on, my son demanded to speak with him. Dan must have asked him five times if he was OK and could he breathe. All my son knew was his father was travelling. He had seen the towers fall and assumed his dada had been nearby. No matter how his father reassured him, he still wasn't convinced of his father's safety.

I set him down to go grab one of his puzzles, a map of the United States. He latched on to me as I got up and wouldn't let me out of his sight. He continued to hold on to my shirttail as he was talking with his father. Luckily, his toybox was just behind the couch. I grabbed the puzzle and we went back and curled up on the couch.

My son had crawled back into my lap and was demanding his dad come over to my house so he could see that he was OK. At this point I finally got my son's attention on the puzzle. I had him place his finger roughly on Albuquerque. Then I showed him where Portland, Oregon was. His father worked for Intel and was out at the main facility for training. I had him place his other finger on Portland, Oregon and slowly dragged it across the board until it came to New York City. I explained to him that the building that fell was all the way across the country and two mountain ranges away from his dad and that he was safe where he was. Seeing the visual finally connected something in his mind. Then he calmly said goodbye to his father and took off to go get dressed. His father tersely explained to me that it had been labeled a terrorist attack. He wondered if the Montessori school was closed and told me no planes were flying. We decided that I would be keeping Dan home that day until we had more information. My ex would not be coming home tonight as planned. Dan and I were on our own. I told his father to be safe and we'd cope until he could get home.

~∿∿∿~

Part of being a good parent is filtering the some-times-harsh reality of the world according to what my child could comprehend. A Middle Eastern terrorist attack in New York, with perhaps more coming—with hundreds if not thousands dead or injured—was beyond his understanding. I wondered if this was the start of WWIII. My house had no basement so there was nothing I could really do now, except stay calm. Panic would have been worse than useless. Dan came running out, dressed in wildly unmatched colors as only a six-year-old could do. He asked with a smile if we could get breakfast on the way to school since we were taking so long to get ready. I sat him down and said that he wouldn't be going to school today, but breakfast out sounded like a good idea. He was not happy about "no school" as he told me there was a cool art project to do today. Breakfast and a promise of watching a dinosaur movie quickly put him in a better frame of mind.

The incidents of September 11th, 2001 brought both abrupt devastation and subtle changes to the psyche of the nation. No adult would ever be able to erase the memories of that day. All of us remember different aspects. I will always remember Dan's trembling and tear tracks glistening in the morning sunlight. He had a few nightmares of dark-skinned people hurting our house and didn't want to let me out of his sight. When his father got home, he slept at my house for a few nights so Dan would sleep better. My Dan was very conflicted about his best friend. He knew Ali's dad looked the same as the terrorists, but he liked Wael. He started waiting with Ali at school until his mom picked him up. Some of the kids had been calling him names because of his ethnicity.

One of the most lasting consequences of that day for my son has been a subtle questioning of safety. When asked, he barely remembers the actual events of the day...just scattered things concerning dad not able to get home and everyone being scared. As he grew up, I noticed he checked out new places in a strange way. When he would start a new grade or school, he would be very concerned about the location. What was the best way out of the building? Did they have a safe place? Sometimes it was even more subtle, the quick turn of his head when we went someplace new, like he was memorizing the exits. All the way through high school he was not fond of new places. He learned a few defensive fighting skills as well. I recognized similar actions with his closet friends. When they were watching movies or gaming at my house, I would hear them talking about how defensible their various houses were. That really shook me. It had been eleven years since the attack and they still talked as if they were consciously preparing for something similar to occur.

~~~

Last year, my son got his own place. It's up in the East Mountains, almost a forty-minute drive from work for him. When I asked him about the location he said, very matter-of-factly, that when, not if, Albuquerque was ever attacked, the Kirtland Air Force Base and Sandia National Laboratory would be prime targets. Living up in the East Mountains would place an entire mountain range between him and the devastation. Therefore, he would be the safe house for his dad, me, and his friends. In the few months he's been living there he told me he's sleeping better, feels less tense, and the dark circles under his eyes have faded. He's more than doubled his commute time, must deal with a cantankerous well, and he still says it's better. His final comment was there are no tall buildings or hordes of people around him, so he finally feels safe.

~~~

It's been almost twenty years since the planes hit, the buildings fell or were destroyed, and thousands of lives were lost. Twenty years of overt threats and postures; fears of unexpected attacks and destruction coming from everyday objects and the man on the street.

But, the subtle changes to those who saw, heard, and internalized the fears may be the most lasting damage of September 11, 2001.

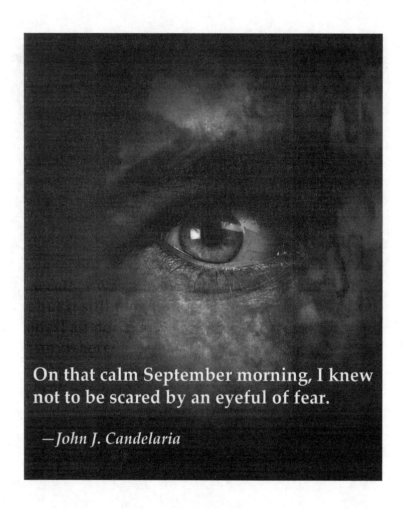

On that calm September morning, I knew
not to be scared by an eyeful of fear.

—*John J. Candelaria*

An Eyeful of Fear

John J. Candelaria

On an undisturbed September morning,
I caught an eyeful of fear from my TV.
Images of exploding airplanes, smoke-filled
towers plummeting in NYC, my birthplace.

Then, the fear increased as the Pentagon
was hit by a third airplane, its western
side in flames. This eyeful was not finished.
A fourth plane plunged into an open field

in Pennsylvania ending these flights
of extreme terror. Media searched for
more visual displays to repeat non-stop
as fear increased among Americans.

This cunning act of terror didn't change
me into a fearful person. Vietnam
tested me earlier, as fear arrived
sometimes daily. That place gave me courage.
A courage to carry on when death paired
with destruction to fill my mind with fright.
I shook off that fear to preserve soldiers'
strength as they too faced trauma and terror.

On that calm September morning, I knew
not to be scared by an eyeful of fear.

It takes intervention to prevent another disaster.

Taking Care of Business

What is the protocol for conducting normal business in the midst of a terrorist attack?

—Loretta Hall

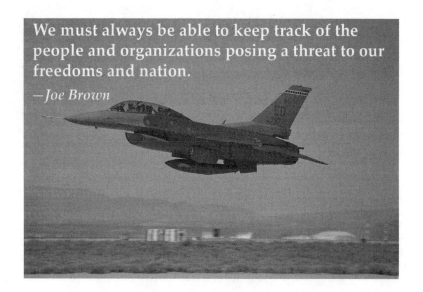

We must always be able to keep track of the people and organizations posing a threat to our freedoms and nation.

—Joe Brown

At Least I Could Do Something About It

Joe Brown

My wife Linda screamed, "Joe, wake up and turn up the TV; you won't believe what just happened." It was barely past 5:45 a.m. PDT in Lancaster, California. I would have only slept another few minutes anyway, but her scream jarred my senses.

I responded, "What's wrong, honey? Are you all right?" I could tell she was distressed more than I had seen in many years.

She said, "Look at the TV and listen." She had been watching NBC's *Today* show as she prepared to go to work. Now Matt Lauer and Katie Couric struggled to keep their composure as they reported what would be the worst tragedy in their lifetimes.

My soul wretched as I experienced the events from moments ago replayed by NBC. I watched a commercial airliner hit the North Tower of the World Trade Center in New York City. Minutes later, I saw another one hit the South Tower. Within an hour-and-a-half, both towers would collapse. Immediately, I was engulfed in anger, grief, and complete disbelief that this could happen here in the United States.

My wife and I were both employed by the United States Air Force (USAF) at Edwards Air Force Base, about thirty miles from our home. Edwards, the home of the Air Force Flight Test Center (AFFTC), remains the largest military installation in the world dedicated to weapons system research and developmental testing. Linda was the Executive Assistant in the Command Section of the Center, directly supporting the Center's Executive Director. At that time, I was a senior USAF civil servant. I directed engineers and project managers executing electronic warfare tests within the Electronic Warfare Directorate (EW) at the AFFTC. A primary role within electronic warfare is to know where your adversary is before he finds you. This puts your enemy at a disadvantage you can exploit. EW tested new capabilities as they were developed.

We scrambled to get to our offices as quickly as possible. As we arrived at the perimeter gate of Edwards, we saw many people directed to turn around. When we got to the gate, the Security Policemen said, "Do you work here at Edwards?"

I responded, "Yes, we both do."

He then said, "Please provide your IDs and step out of your car."

We were allowed into the base following a search of our vehicle and confirmation of our identity. Security had immediately changed from routine operating procedures, which were stringent, to the level necessary to support a war effort.

Arriving at the secure compound where my office was located, I learned from the security guard at the gate into the area that the Pentagon was under attack.

Entering the office suite, my secretary said through

her tears, "You have a caller on your secure line."

I replied, "Thanks, has he been waiting long? Are you OK?"

She managed to say, "I'm OK, and no, it has only been a minute or two."

The caller was my buddy, Bill Stillwater, from the Center "Intel" office. He stated, "We are being ordered to stand ready to support a response to another attack. Come to the secure conference room at 3 p.m. today. The Pentagon has scheduled a video teleconference to discuss today's events. Headquarters Air Force apprised us. They've launched F-16 fighters along the east coast. The pilots are to attack any aircraft identified as non-responsive to air traffic controllers and not following an approved flight plan."

I said, "I'll see you later." Then I sat for a while in the quiet refuge of my office. Emotions surfaced—focused anger, determination, conviction, and things I hadn't felt for a decade. I was a retired Air Force Non-Commissioned Officer on 9/11, and it had been ten years since my Desert Storm deployment to Germany.

We had not expected a terrorist problem in Nuremberg, but that is what we faced daily. I was unarmed because of my assignment to a medical unit. The terrorists did not respect the Geneva Convention Rules of Engagement, which stipulate that medical staff are non-combatants. But I had vivid memories of being targeted multiple times in Germany by Syrian terrorists supporting Saddam Hussein in 1991. It happened on four separate occasions, resulting in car chases and being shot at during my duty. Heroic last-minute action saved the entire medical unit from being blown up by a suicide bomber carrying a satchel of C-4 plastic explosives. Fortunately, several members of the aircraft maintenance crew assigned to support our operation tackled the terrorist as he came within twenty-five yards of our location. After being the target of terrorists, I developed a strong appreciation for the dedication they have in support of their cause.

Those visions raced through my mind and created the emotions I was feeling as I prepared to attend the meeting at the secure conference room on 9/11.

My position at the AFFTC required security clearances that went beyond top-secret. The Air Force employed me, but my work often supported or was driven by information coming from the Intelligence community. The "Intel" office kept my security records in a vault at their site. I would support the response to this crisis using my relationships within the Department of Defense (DoD) test community, the Intelligence Community (CIA, NSA, FBI etc.), and the various members of the DoD industrial world.

Later that day, Bill called, "Get up here as soon as you can; the video conference start time has been moved up." I dropped what I was doing and gathered my briefcase, placing my notes and recent testing data from my test site in it.

I arrived at the classified conference room before the meeting started. I took a seat in the second row directly behind the AFFTC Commander, Major General (Two-Star) Doug Patterson. When the video came up, we saw a conference room in the Pentagon like ours at Edwards. The Joint Chiefs of Staff were visible along with the Secretary of the Air Force and others I recognized from past meetings. The speaker was from the intelligence community, and you could see stress written all over his face. He began, "We have already determined the instigators of the offensive earlier today were terrorists from the Middle East. We will confirm soon precisely who the individual participants were."

The speaker continued with his voice trembling, "We also identified where we fell short in accurately analyzing the immediate threat these individuals and the organizations supporting them posed."

The AFFTC Commander was openly showing untypical emotion. His left hand held a pencil he randomly tapped on the arm of his chair. He abruptly interrupted the briefer. With a passionate voice, he said, "Provide detail regarding your last statement. You say we fell short in our intelligence analysis. How and why did this happen?"

The speaker sensed the General's passion and concern. He cleared his throat and thoughtfully responded, "Within the decade leading up to today, the intelligence community and the defense department lost funding. That meant they were unable to keep their experienced personnel and to pay for equipment upgrades. This loss drastically affected their capabilities. General, as you know, there are several tools that are used to collect and analyze intelligence data. Most experts in this field agree intelligence data gathered by humans is the most reliable. It costs more to collect, but it is the data that is the most complete and accurate. It can be delivered quickly to the appropriate agency and put into use." He concluded, "Sir, that is the area of intelligence that was hit hardest in this past decade."

By 2001, I had held my top-secret security clearances for twenty-eight years. During that time, I saw organizations within our defense and intelligence communities ebb and flow regarding their staff size and budget. The information he had shared came as no surprise to me.

The speaker continued and shared all the confirmed information available. Then the leaders at the Pentagon stated that we in the field were to prepare information regarding our readiness to address a war effort anywhere in the world. This was to be delivered within forty-eight hours. Obviously, we knew the Middle East was in the picture, but now we knew even our homeland could be vulnerable.

Following the briefing, the general turned and said, "Joe, I need you and Col. K to meet me in an hour in my office. We need to discuss our action items from this meeting. You are the two people I know who have been analyzing and planning against an adversary like this."

Col. K was Col. George Kellough, at that time the Commandant of the USAF Test Pilot School. He, like myself, was a charter member of the Electronic Warfare Directorate (EW). Col. K and I had previously created the "Roadmap" for that Directorate. The Directorate followed the roadmap in making improvements to its test capabilities.

The General wanted to know what we saw as the first concerns the AFFTC needed to address. He asked, "What are our key capabilities we'll use immediately to address our country's military response?"

Col. K said, "Anything we can use as testers to validate and improve surveillance and detection capabilities in finding our adversary. We also must enhance our ability to detect where they have placed Improvised Explosive Devices (IEDS) along roads our troops will use."

"We must be able to test and confirm our ability to intercept our adversary's communications and test and improve our ability to encrypt our communications," I said. Then I added, "Efficiently capturing their information and safely sharing ours will improve our effectiveness."

The General responded, "Great thoughts, and now I need you to discuss these with the planners at the Pentagon. Combine their ideas with yours and report back to me. We'll then layout your assignments so you and your teams can create solutions."

After meeting with the General, I returned to the EW Directorate and found Col. Steve Hansen. He was the organization's Director (Commander). I wanted to share what was discussed in the General's office. As I entered Hansen's office, he said, "Joe, let's sit over here at my conference table."

We had known each other over ten years, going back to when I was a Tech Sgt. and he was a Major. Steve was my best umpire when I served as President of Edward's Little League baseball. Having known each other on the job as professionals and within the Edwards community as parents and volunteers, we were uniquely prepared to use that trusting relationship to quickly and effectively address a critically important matter facing our country.

We each had notes from the briefing at "Intel." I looked up from mine and spat out the words, "Steve, I can't believe this has happened. How could we not have seen this coming?"

I heard anger in his voice as he replied, "Joe, our intel community has suffered over the past two administrations. They were gutted. Reagan built it up, and that led to the fall of the Wall and the Soviet Union. We in the military have also suffered; our equipment is getting older and harder to maintain at the readiness level we need."

Sharing crooked smiles, we looked at each other and silently agreed to quit whining and focus on doing something special.

Steve said, "Joe, as the project manager who created the Benefield Anechoic Facility and is now its Chief of Test Operations, how should we use that place immediately?"

I replied, "Let's finish the testing we have started

on the new CV-22 Osprey. It's currently in the facility and we can wrap that up in one more week. Then let's schedule representative air vehicles with our most advanced sensors for a quick-look test on each. That will confirm what we think we know about each of them. That information will be valuable to U.S. Central Command (CENTCOM) planners as they prepare to deploy our assets. We also need to verify what testing we currently support across the Center. We can identify what we need to continue and even accelerate. Certainly, we'll have to reprioritized some projects out of the current picture."

Everything we were doing on 9/10 was necessary, but as of 9/11, new immediate threats existed, and therefore new priorities for our resources, which were limited, would be developed.

Those discussions started our efforts, and we moved forward as fast as we possibly could to address what had happened earlier that day.

I cannot share the specific decisions and steps taken, but they directly impacted me and Col. K. over the next twenty-four months. The real action started as I undertook special projects driven by what happened on 9/11, and Col. K was involved with many of them. He decided to retire from the USAF and accept a new position as Technical Advisor to the AFFTC Commander. He had a Ph.D., and would become known as Dr. K. or George, but most importantly, he became critical to the AFFTC responding effectively to the needs of the USAF.

Dr. K arrived at his new office, saw my wife, and said, "Linda, am I going to be working with both Browns?"

She laughed and replied, "Aren't you the lucky one?"

He grinned and said, "Yes, I guess I am."

I also moved into a planning role within the Center staff. I would advise the General. My new office was downstairs from the Command Section. It only took a minute or two to get up there when needed.

George and I often traveled together for the next several years, attending many planning meetings across the country for the USAF and the DoD. We supported tactical and strategic planning, sitting on panels with experts from across the military services. We addressed 9/11, but we also discussed other potential military vulnerabilities and how we could efficiently and effectively correct them.

We became a formidable team and worked exceptionally well together.

My Desert Storm experience amplified my desire to do all I could to make sure "9/11" never happened again. As an Air Force civil servant, I was grateful to be part of the team supporting efforts to protect American citizens from any future terrorist attack.

From September of 2001 until June of 2010 when I retired, almost all my time was spent as part of groups of senior DoD leaders determining the requirements the test community must meet to prepare our military to defend our country against possible threats. I assisted the AFFTC commander and his peers across the Air Force in finding the resources to apply toward those threats. We learned much from those efforts, and those lessons learned would be used for years to come as the intelligence and military communities worked in tandem to keep Americans safe at home and around the world.

~ων~

On 9/11, I was devastated by the loss of innocent lives on our soil. We will never know, but I believed then and still do today, that we likely could have avoided the tragedy. We must always be able to keep track of the people and organizations posing a threat to our freedoms and nation. On September 11, 2001 we knew, in general, who they were. Because of the cuts in funding, we did not have the resources to keep constant track of their activities. We have addressed this problem since then.

Sadly, for thousands of people—the victims of that day and their loved ones—the correction came too late and at far too high a price.

Luckily the weather was good over most of the country, but it still took hours to get them [airplanes] all down and parked somewhere, anywhere.

—*Rose Marie Kern*

Grounded

Rose Marie Kern

The entire Air Traffic Control system and aviation community were rocked by events on the day terrorists flew two aircraft into the World Trade Center, and another one into the Pentagon. A startling message flashed through the system to every facility around the country—LAND ALL AIRCRAFT IMMEDIATELY.

A startled disbelief was belayed instantly by phone communications with Washington, D.C. Controllers on break watching television news were called away from the horrifying pictures of aircraft hitting the twin towers to begin implementing the first stages of the federal emergency procedures.

The twenty-two Air Traffic Control Centers which monitor the airspace over the Continental U.S., Alaska, and Hawaii immediately began the process needed to land over 4,500 commercial and private aircraft. Center controllers working the Air Defense Identification Zone (ADIZ), which defines our country's borders aloft, had to turn aircraft away.

The first few hours were crazy as controllers in the big Air Route Traffic Control Centers (ARTCC) and local Air Traffic Control Towers directed thousands of aircraft to land. The FAA notified all the air carriers that they must find places outside the U.S. to land incoming aircraft. People flying home from vacations found themselves landing in Canada, Mexico, or Greenland. Some of the aircraft turned back to their departure points.

Luckily the weather was good over most of the country, but it still took hours to get them all down and parked somewhere, anywhere. The Centers had to look for airports capable of handling the various types of aircraft...you can't land a Boeing 747 at any airport with a runway less than a mile and a half long!

Most people were aware that the air carriers were grounded—many of them far from their destinations, many of them outside the borders of the United States. We heard about those people and their experience through mass media. But the order included everything that was in flight—corporate jets, small general aviation aircraft, helicopters, hot air balloons, gliders, and ultralights.

Those first few hours were frenetic. No one was on break; all the knowledge, skills and experiences each person had accumulated though their careers were needed to make sure each aircraft was routed to the closest airport adequate to its needs. The carefully woven pathways which make up the fabric of our nation's air traffic system were skillfully pulled apart as one by one the aircraft touched earth.

While most aircraft were being forced to land, the military bases across the nation were gearing up. Daily routine training flights were cancelled and airmen called back from leave. The New Mexico Air National

Guard fleet of F16s, affectionately known as the "Enchilada Air Force" were assigned strategic routes across the southwestern United States.

The three Air Force bases in New Mexico sent aloft aircraft with specific defense initiatives. Canon AFB out of Clovis participated in defense of the southern ADIZ. Kirtland AFB scrambled fighters and aircraft with equipment to monitor the northern half of the state, specifically around Los Alamos and Sandia National Laboratories. Holloman AFB watched the southern half, including White Sands Missile Range, White Sands Space Harbor, and the NASA test facility.

That morning I was sleeping after a midnight shift at the Albuquerque Air Traffic Control Flight Service Station (FSS) when my daughter, Melissa, woke me and had me turn on the television. Like everyone else in the U.S., I was stunned by the willful devastation.

After the initial rush to land aircraft, the ARTCC and Tower personnel had little to do as only military, law enforcement, and emergency aircraft were allowed to fly for a couple weeks. There is only one published phone number into the air traffic system which anyone can readily request from directory assistance, and which pilots memorize from day one of flight training: 1-800-WXBRIEF. This is the nationwide phone number going to the Flight Service Stations.

This is the division of ATC in which I was working at the time. During the weeks after 9/11, specialists in

FSS operations nationally took thousands of calls hourly from pilots who only had one question: "When can we fly?"

Being a border station, the Albuquerque FSS where I worked juggled hundreds of calls primarily from pilots stuck in Mexico and points south. These included U.S. citizens coming back from holiday, as well as business aircraft flying products from the maquiladoras (manufacturing plants) to the U.S. Even on the ground, border patrols were stopping, and much more keenly inspecting trucks filled with seat covers or wiring harnesses destined for the auto manufacturing plants in Detroit. Without those items, factories would have to slow down or stop production lines.

I took calls from parents needing to get home to their children, aging parents, and jobs. A call came in from someone whose Mom had had a heart attack. Though they raged and cried, the only option I could offer was for them to fly to one of the border airports on the Mexican side where they had to leave their aircraft and take a bus over the border and make their way north from there.

The Federal Aviation Administration (FAA) allowed aircraft to take flight in stages. After a couple days the first civilian group to be given a green light was the agricultural field-spraying aircraft. The USDA implored the FAA to allow them to continue this time-critical action as it could affect the nation's food supply long term.

Unfortunately, as soon as the general public saw these low altitude aircraft spraying chemicals over the area, they started calling in a panic. "Terrorists are spraying poisons!" So, the Ag planes were grounded for another couple days, then released again.

After a week, the large air carriers were given permission to resume flights, followed by the other corporate and shipping entities. After two weeks general aviation within the country was almost back to normal, but any aircraft caught outside U.S. airspace wanting to come in was still blocked whether there were American citizens involved or not. With heavy military patrols along the Air Defense Identification Zone, nobody wanted to risk trying to get home under the radar! It took at least five weeks before the system approached normal conditions.

In the aftermath of 9/11, most civilians noted those changes to air travel which involved them personally — heightened security procedures at airports, and less access to flight crews. The long-term repercussions to Air Traffic involved heavier security at all ATC facilities, the creation of new restricted airspaces, and new procedures in heavily flown areas.

In the past, pilots could call an ATC facility and easily arrange tours for themselves, school groups, student pilots, and families. Now, all visitors to an ATC facility must be approved prior to entering. ARTCC and Tower facilities now require each person's personal information be submitted to and approved by Homeland Security a couple weeks prior to visits.

Flight Service (FSS) has always been the branch of

Air Traffic Control to which pilots had the greatest access. The new regulations made things difficult for local general aviation pilots who customarily visited FSS facilities for services they'd used for decades. Although technology had improved to the point that pilots could get their pre-flight briefings and file their flight plans over the phone, many would walk from the airport ramp into an FSS—if there was one on the airfield—and look at the weather graphics as well as talk to a professional weather and flight briefer about anything that might affect their upcoming travel.

After 9/11, they could no longer just amble in the front door of the Albuquerque FSS. They had to ring the bell for a security guard to let them in the Operations room. Because we were a low risk facility, after a while the doors were modified so pilots could come straight into Operations, but they could not access anywhere else.

Nonetheless, since that time pilots have migrated away from personal interaction with the FSS specialists, and learned to use more distant options. The FAA consolidated all the smaller facilities into two larger ones nationwide which now do all the pilot briefings either online, over the radio, or by phone. Although there are still ARTCC and Tower facilities in Albuquerque, the ABQ Flight Service facility was closed in 2008.

Rose Marie Kern worked in all three branches of Air Traffic Control during her thirty-four-year career. A modified version of this story first appeared in her memoir, *Stress is Relative*, currently available from Amazon.

...spirits dropping from the sky - no way to unremember...

—Sylvia Ramos Cruz

Smoke billowed from the building, and I presumed it was a technical programming error, but no matter what I tried, it wouldn't change.

—*Pete Christensen*

LIVE

BREAKING NEWS

Divide or Conquer?

Pete Christensen

On September 11, 2001, I was finishing my shift as a master control operator at an Albuquerque TV station at around 8:45 a.m. Suddenly, the program I was monitoring went black and traffic cameras appeared. It was a large metropolitan area, but exactly where I couldn't be sure. Then, the cameras began to move in a jerky, mechanical sort of way until they were aimed at the World Trade Center. Oddly enough, I recognized it from the 1976 version of *King Kong*, starring Jeff Bridges.

Smoke billowed from the building, and I presumed it was a technical programming error, but no matter what I tried, it wouldn't change. (I now know the Emergency Broadcast System had been implemented). My replacement appeared five minutes early for his shift, around 8:55 a.m. He told me someone flew a plane into the building. I imagined it was some misguided student in a single engine Piper Cub, or some hapless private jet executive flight.

We watched in shock and amazement as the crawl at the bottom of the screen read out that a major airliner had been hijacked and struck the building at over 400 miles an hour. At around 9:05 a.m., a second plane en-

73

tered the picture and seemed to fly in back of the second tower. When it disappeared from view, my co-worker yelled out "Oh my God, I think that plane just crashed into that other building!" Soon after the chief engineer called and instructed us to go to programming from our other area station, an NBC affiliate.

The details unfolded slowly while the devastation revealed itself immediately. We both sat mesmerized by the quickly updated reports. The carnage and conspiracies seemed endless and the possibilities of future attacks seemed unavoidable. (I later learned from a taped interview from Osama Bin Laden that he never expected the United States to ground all air traffic instantly. THAT, it turns out may have saved thousands more).

Suddenly I snapped out of my transfixed state and realized I needed to go home and break this news to my wife, who'd no doubt still be sleeping. When I got home, I sat on the edge of our bed and looked at her sleeping peacefully. What I was going to tell her would possibly change her view of the world forever and shatter the peaceful existence she inhabited.

I put a hand on her shoulder and waited for her to awake. As she looked up, I told her all I knew, and all anybody knew at that time. "The country is under attack on the East Coast, but nobody seems to know yet by who, and why."

Like people driving slowly past a car accident, we were transfixed on the news events as we watched history unfold around us. Any fear we had was overcome by curiosity. Who was attacking us? Was this just the start of the aggression? How bad was the butchery and destruction going to be? The television information was varied, and somewhat confusing. There were reports of three hijackings, but they had not been confirmed. It still wasn't clear if they were even related.

There were few words exchanged between us. I truly wished for the eloquence to say something strong, yet reassuring, but as is the case in these situations, the words eluded me. I don't remember how long we watched in silence, but it seemed like noon, our time, when the first tower collapsed. There it was, live on network television, a stunned world-wide audience witnessing the death of thousands, just as easily as if we were watching a sporting event. My stomach fell nauseous. I was still in disbelief as the skyscraper seemed to collapse in slow motion. We looked at each other and she talked in a whisper so soft that if I hadn't watched her lips, I wouldn't have known what she said.

"Oh my God, this is actually happening."

I just nodded in agreement.

Literally just moments went by when it was announced another hijacked plane had crashed in a field near Shanksville, Pennsylvania, killing all aboard.

Years earlier, I was a radio newsman in Wisconsin when reports came across the Associated Press late one night about a mass suicide in Guyana, at a place called Jonestown. Throughout that night I watched the wire service as the death toll climbed. I felt a tinge of *déjà vu* as again, I sat helpless as the casualties crept higher.

～∾∿∾～

A half hour passed when the North tower collapsed with a reported 1,600 people still trapped inside. I had finished an eight-hour shift and had been in front of the television for five more, but my hunger was quelled by sudden realization that I had friends working in New York City. How close were they to Ground Zero? Should I call them? Would a call get in the way of their being contacted by relatives? In retrospect, it was so very odd that in a time of tragedy, I was concerned with etiquette. Perhaps that's what it means to be human, to be aware of others and your effect on them, even in the slightest of ways, and at the cruelest of times.

As the sun set on that day, I sat on my back porch looking out, aware of the desert's stillness. I sipped on my coffee. *This is my generation's Pearl Harbor.*

That tragic day will forever hold us together in a single event. A mark of our character will be whether that bond remains strong, or if we allow it to create division among us.

My Desert Storm experience amplified my desire to do all I could to make sure "9/11" never happened again.

—Joe Brown

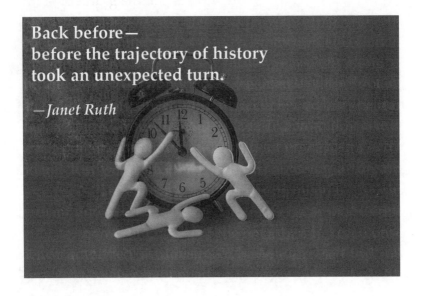

Back before—
before the trajectory of history
took an unexpected turn.

—*Janet Ruth*

Counting Backward Toward Before

Janet Ruth

We bring back
the troops, put down
missiles and rifles, withdraw
fearful, suspicious stares
from fellow humans on planes,
in public places—Middle Eastern
faces that could be Moses
or Jesus or Mohammed.

Watching television, tears
roll up our cheeks, hands
uncover our faces. On a morning
like any other we return
to what we had been doing—
eating breakfast, morning exercises,
getting in the car to drive to work.

And the twin towers
swallow smoke and flames.
People run backward into coffee shops,
sit down to newspapers folded open,
mugs of cooling latte.
They jog backward to catch taxis
that slowly reverse into the day.
As the cloud of dust and smoke is sucked
back into ground level at the towers,

first responders back out, remove their gear.
People walk back into buildings,
help each other up stairwells,
sit down at their desks, take a moment
to call husband or wife or child to say
I love you and *I'll see you tonight for dinner*—
fingers click on keyboards.

Tourists in the street watch
glass and debris rise up from pavement
like dirty rain falling up,
stare as bodies flap skyward
like pigeons back to window ledges.
Towers reemerge, reconstruct themselves
like the Phoenix from her ashes.
The World Trade Center is whole,
and 2,997 more people are alive.

As the New York horizon regains
two pylons that hold up the sky,
those towers expel two airplanes.
The pilots of flights #11 and #175
sit up, lift their hands to the controls,
swing their planes back toward Boston.
Inside the planes' cabins
passengers refasten seatbelts—
clinking carts roll down the aisles with coffee.
Five men on each plane close cockpit doors,
return to their seats, return something dark
to their jacket pockets.
When the planes land, all disembark.

The anonymous non-perpetrators—
no carryon bags, no checked luggage—
back away, disappear below the surface
of the sea of Tuesday morning airport faces.

We are not yet looking for someone to blame,
someone upon whom to exact revenge.
Back before—
before the trajectory of history
took an unexpected turn.

Understanding 9/11 is a long and difficult process. And we cannot let such attacks happen again.

Making Sense of It

That tragic day will forever hold us together in a single event. A mark of our character will be whether that bond remains strong, or if we allow it to create division among us.

—Pete Christensen

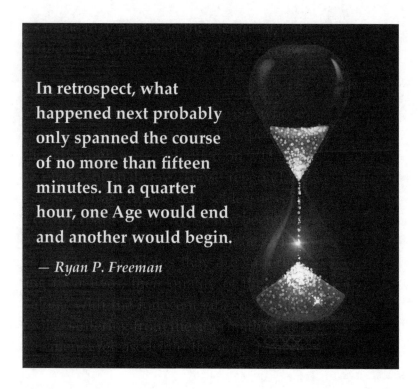

In retrospect, what happened next probably only spanned the course of no more than fifteen minutes. In a quarter hour, one Age would end and another would begin.

— *Ryan P. Freeman*

That One September Day

Ryan P. Freeman

That one September, I remember waking up to TV. You know the space your brain makes when there's something from outside—something from waking life—mixing with your dreams? That's what it was like. Back then I was in middle school. Our family home was on a corner lot right behind the high school. My room faced the Sandia Mountains which tower over Albuquerque's sometimes twinkling, always bustling cityscape. As I slowly emerged from a now-forgotten dream, the vague idea entered my mind that there was some sort of B action movie playing downstairs. Still not awake, I padded down our long hallway to the top of the stairs.

The house had an open floorplan. This meant I could hear the rest of my family clattering around the kitchen and table. Spoons, bowls, cereal, milk, toast. The casual murmur of another middle-class American family gathering for the day. A work day for some. A school day for others like my sisters and me. Our home's open floor plan also meant I could finally see whatever was playing on TV from my perch atop the stairs.

It still looked like some generic movie destined for ignominy. A solid box office flop. A camera panned across a city skyline awash with morning sun. Smoke (or was it just haze) drifted across the panorama. In the distance, I thought I could make out the Statue of Liberty, dark green and stalwart as ever, staring unblinking into the rising sun.

The thought mumbled through my groggy mind that this was not a movie I had seen before. I rounded the tiled kitchen counter. Found a clean bowl. Filled it with cereal and milk. Found a spoon of my own. Most of my family sat on the couch, eyes glued to the screen.

Odd. My parents were usually dogmatic in their insistence that we keep the TV off while eating together.

"What's this?" I asked.

"They just flew a plane into the World Trade Center," replied someone.

Now crunching on breakfast, I pulled up dusty memories. Maybe it was from *Die Hard II*? Unsure, I continued eating and watching, transfixed with the rest. Medusa herself could not have paralyzed my family any better. As I ate, I began waking up in earnest—a trait I still keep today.

In retrospect, what happened next probably only spanned the course of no more than fifteen minutes. In a quarter hour, one Age would end and another would begin. One entire Zeitgeist would fade before the arrival of another. Those who have been born after won't understand. Before, the power going out was exciting. Now, not so much. Before, when planes were in the news (for it was the news I now realized I was watching), it was some accident. Things righted themselves. The sun shone. Things were still generally good and right.

I can't tell you how I knew. But I did. Now awake, I looked on with the rest of the world as cameras switched from one angle to another at the gaping crater pocking one of the towers. I watched and somehow, I knew this wasn't an accident—never mind how much my older sister and mom insisted otherwise.

As if on some prophetic cue, a second plane appeared. I knew what was going to happen. My stomach dropped like a stone, carrying my freshly-eaten cereal with it, milk and all.

Two towers. Two planes.

And while the commentators conjectured, I watched. Haunted by weird foreknowledge guided by cold logic, I watched. I remember watching the second plane as it flew straight at the second tower. To this day, whenever I see old news reels or shaky handheld videos made off of those sturdy Nokia brick phones, I wonder about what those last thirty seconds were like for those aboard. To this day.

It makes me angry and sick. Strong emotions for an eighth grader.

I think the silence that followed was so loud. So loud it deafened hearts and reason and the fabric of the sort of story we had, up until that point, been confidently telling ourselves about Life, the Universe, and Everything. That's how loud it was.

I don't remember the rest of that morning. What I do remember is staring at another TV in math class a little later. My parents had decided to send me to school, despite rumors flying that nowhere was safe. I remember sitting in those hard Formica-topped metal desks with the uncomfortable plastic seats. Except that day, I never noticed how much sitting in them hurt. I was too busy hurting about real things to complain about the mundane.

~~∽ର୧∽~~

When the commentator announced another plane had been spotted, possibly heading toward the White House, I saw inevitable images in my head playing out. I hoped the live news cameras would avoid the tiny dots of business people jumping to their deaths from skyscrapers. I was maybe thirteen. But the plane changed course and went for the Pentagon, instead (as if that was any better?).

It didn't matter which room we were shuffled to or from all that day at school. A TV mounted in the corner, the ones usually resigned to playing student news programs about baseball practice and cheerleading tryouts or band practice had all decided together they would broadcast something entirely else that day.

I know I somehow wound up at home again. All day, I remember people waiting for something else to happen, but nothing really did. Everyone tried to make sure everyone else was safe. Despite the busy signals, we just kept calling until we got through.

Numbed, my family drove to church. Normally, on a Sunday, our place of worship was about three-quarters full. This time, on a random weekday evening it was packed. Standing-room-only filled with mostly people I had never seen before. Strangers. Americans all. That night, as the candles flickered and the prayers rose, we sang together like we meant it. Like things mattered. Like we cared. Because we did and perhaps because deep down, we still do…and that's why we all get so mad about things that really don't matter compared to that day in September. We really are one people. Deep down, our differences can unite us.

Afterward, not too few of us wondered how long the Feeling would linger. But, slowly, it faded. The President was on TV more often. Stocks plummeted (not that I really cared). Some time later, I watched as squadrons of sleek black stealth bombers took off from the nearby air base. Another country exploded in flames and terror. It seemed as if the violence we experienced was carried on in another place, far away. Some place on the edge of the map I had never heard of, except on a Risk® map.

I don't think about all of this anymore. The memories are tucked away, neat and orderly, somewhere in my mind where I never go. A box in a mental attic. The last solid memory I have of that day in September was when Brian Jennings came on again later that evening. On live news, he told his country that he had no words to say. For once, the shiny veneer for which I've later come to hold against newscasters peeled back. Underneath, a real living, breathing, hurting human being looked back out at me.

I'm not a stranger to death. I'm a cancer survivor who

has been medically dead for over five minutes on multiple occasions. All the same, I remember things that give you that sort of perspective. Those sorts of things which give you a glimpse from some other higher ground where clarity is not quite as scarce as it is down in the lowlands of everyday living.

Many years later, I met another sort of survivor. At my dad's church I would let people in on Sunday morning. Located in an apartment complex, the exterior door to the parking lot automatically locked, if shut. It was up to me to recognize who was coming for church and who wasn't (Oh, how the world had already changed. A swiftly tilting planet if ever I'd known one). An old lady would come down every Sunday morning. Full of spite and vinegar, she would make pointed comments at me until she either tired or the music began and I could make an exit as gracefully as socially appropriate.

It wasn't for several months until I noticed her tattoo. Holocaust survivor.

Before she passed away of old age and unremitted grief, she told me two things. One was how she thought the best thing that could happen to America now was for us to be invaded, so people would learn on the spot what actually mattered. The second thing she told me after years of sharp-tongued comments was that I was a good boy, and that she liked me.

Too often, we worry about 9/11 decorum when really, we need to be around other Americans. Especially

Americans who aren't like us. We need to experience someone else's need and feel someone else's heartbreak. We need to Know we share something which transcends the indelible bonds of personhood. We need to know we are something together which we are not and cannot be apart. We are all Americans.

It just took one day in September to remind us, is all.

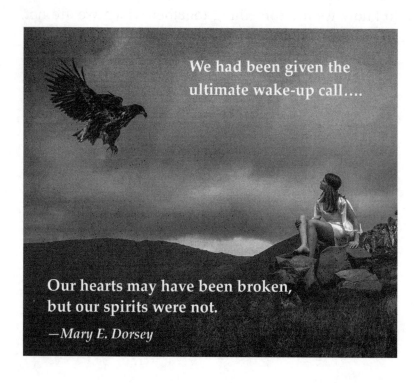

We had been given the ultimate wake-up call....

Our hearts may have been broken, but our spirits were not.

—*Mary E. Dorsey*

September

Mary E. Dorsey

That Tuesday began a normal, beautiful New Mexico late summer morning. The sky, the vivid, startling blue that New Mexicans know so well. A few clouds, wispy and white, painted the brilliant blue background. The air was warm with just a hint of the chill that would soon arrive.

I was getting ready for work. Already showered and dressed, I prepared my breakfast and turned on the TV. Immediately I knew something was wrong. Katie Couric's normally smiling face was grim. On the screen, in the background two buildings were on fire. It took a moment for me to realize those tall buildings were the Twin Towers—the iconic symbol of the New York skyline. What at first appeared to be a tragic accident soon became a tragedy all its own. I stared silently at what was unfolding on my TV screen: the recap showing the first plane hitting the North Tower, and then, minutes later, the second plane slicing through the metal and glass of the South Tower like a fiery death sword. My spoonful of cereal froze between bowl and mouth. Whether it made it to its destination I still cannot remember.

My eyes were glued to the screen in both horror and fascination, transfixed as I watched fire, smoke, and bits of debris rain down upon the street. It wasn't until much later that I realized some of that debris was actually people making an unthinkable choice: be burned alive or jump, hoping that somehow, someway, they would sprout wings before crashing into the concrete below. My heart had already sunk as I prayed for those people trapped above the inferno and for those I hoped would get out before the unthinkable could happen. Were those towers strong enough to withstand the onslaught? Would they collapse?

At some point, I realized I needed to get to my school nurse job and reluctantly turned off the television. I brushed my teeth, washed my breakfast dishes, then drove the short distance to work. The first thing I saw when I walked in was the secretary, her face sad and tear-streaked.

"The Towers....?" My question trailed off.

"Collapsed." Was her simple answer.

"Both?" I responded.

All she could do was nod her head "Yes" before dissolving into tears. I stood stunned, too numb, too heartbroken to cry. My mind kept thinking about the people, both those working in the towers and the responders courageously coming to their aid. These people had begun their day as if it were like any other yet they would not be going home that evening...not ever going home. Their families, their friends would never see them again. My mind could not comprehend so many lives shattered because of such unbelievable acts of hatred and violence. People trapped, forced to make an unthinkable, unbearable choice. Did they manage to get to safety before the collapse? Were they buried under rubble so deep they could never be recovered? Everything seemed too much to bear and…it wasn't over.

The news that a third plane had hit the Pentagon, killing even more innocent lives, would add to the heartbreak, anger, outrage, fear, and bewilderment.

The final blow came a bit later when, in a field over Shanksville, Pennsylvania, thirty-three passengers, two pilots, and five flight attendants of United Flight 93 became unwitting yet courageous heroes.

With two words, "Let's roll," they thwarted the four hijackers on board in what was to be the final attack. That plane's target, speculated to be the White House or Capitol Building, would not complete its heinous mission. Instead, the brave people on that flight gave their lives to stop the hijackers. The plane crashed into an empty field which will forever be a testament to unselfish courage. All these attacks became more than what we the people could bear. Questions flowed from lips, but no one had an answer.

WHY? WHO? HOW? WHY? Why would someone do this to us? Who could do such a thing to U.S.? How could this have happened? We are the United States of America! The greatest country on earth! It seemed like an awful nightmare.

But it wasn't a nightmare.

I don't know how much work I got done that day, if any…how much anyone got done that day. I do remember this was not the first time I'd felt such helpless vulnerability, such utter shock at another act of violence against our country. It had been nearly thirty-eight years since, on a lovely fall day, the innocent tranquility of 1963 was shattered by an assassin's bullet. I was a sixteen-year-old sophomore living in Stratford, Connecticut, riding the school bus home. It was around 2:45 p.m. Eastern time, which made it 1:45 p.m. in Dallas, Texas. Many of the students on the bus had been dropped off, so I had a seat all to myself. Across the aisle from me sat a junior known for her jokes. Suddenly she looked up from her transistor radio and said, "The president's been shot."

Those near her said something like "Yeah, right."

A few minutes later she looked right at me and said. "The president's dead. They're playing the national anthem." She shoved the radio in my direction. I couldn't make out exactly what was playing but I knew it wasn't the usual teen music. It seemed like it was the national anthem and that President Kennedy really was dead. The rest of the ride home was silent. When we got to our stop, my sister, Sue, and I raced home. We burst into the house and stopped dead in our tracks. Instead of the usual Jessie Brewer and Doctor Steve of General Hospital, there was Walter Cronkite struggling to tell a stunned country the president had been murdered. Our mom was in the kitchen, crying, and we could do nothing but wonder, "How could this happen in America?" What had once been a teenage sense of invulnerability became a frightening attack on our safety, our way of thinking, believing, living, on all we had once taken for granted and was now, forever gone.

It all came flooding back on 9/11. But this time, it was even worse. So many innocent lives were lost in a short a period of time. It was such a calculated act of violence. No one could have anticipated or prepared for this kind of attack. If no one could have prepared for or defended this, what could anyone do to stop it from happening again? That thought may have been the most frightening, terrifying of all. Who, when, where will it happen next?

Yet…we are a resilient country. A strong country. We may bend, but we will not be broken. We will rise from the ashes of tragedy to rebuild. Our hearts may have been broken, but our spirits were not.

During my daily walks I realized everything had changed. With all flights cancelled, there was an eerie silence. The drone of engines, a sound that was hardly noticed before, now was a glaring absence. The TV provided nearly constant coverage of the lives lost, who they were, what they did, and what their loss meant to friends, family, and country. Soon we were told about those responsible and how they carried out their maniacal plot. And, to our national relief, hopefully, we could prevent something like this from ever happening again.

The Patriot Act had quickly become law. At airports, we had to trade speed and convenience for a slower, more deliberate process. The ease of life we had become accustomed to now had an edge. We were less complacent, more wary. Our cocoon of trust and contentment had been shattered. America had been attacked by strangers who hated everything we stood for, and we could never go back to the way it was before.

We had been given the ultimate wake-up call.

At some point, the monumental task of cleaning up began. At the World Trade Center site, it would take months to remove the nearly two million tons of rubble from what had once been a thriving community. On May 30, 2002 the last beam, one from the South Tower, was removed. Draped in a simple, black shroud and accompanied by a single stretcher draped in an American flag, symbolic of all who had lost their lives, it was given an honor guard escort. It was a hero's farewell for nearly three thousand people needlessly slaughtered that day in New York, Washington, D.C., and Pennsylvania, including the brave responders who rushed to their aid.

That beam was housed in an abandoned airplane hangar until August 24, 2006 when it was returned to its former home. A new, beautiful, skyscraper, called The Freedom Tower, stands close to where the Twin Towers once dominated lower Manhattan.

There is a memorial where the Towers once stood. Smooth, dark granite surrounds twin pools set in the footprints of those once mighty buildings. On the parapet's surrounding those pools, inscribed in bronze, are the names of the nearly three thousand people lost on that day, along with those lost on February 26, 1993 — the first attack on the Twin Towers. It's a place for visitors and loved ones of the fallen to remember, meditate, and worship; a place for all to read and touch the names of those who were lost on that day, those who gave the ultimate sacrifice. It is an uncommon place, yet one of reverence and beauty. That beam is on permanent display in the museum on that site. It is there to remind everyone of that dreadful day and to make sure that we, indeed, never forget.

~∽∾∽~

There is one name missing from that memorial. That name is Sirius. He was a four-year old Yellow Lab, a member of the K-9 unit. He, along with his handler, David Lim, worked for the Port Authority of New York and New Jersey. They were Explosive Detectors. On that fateful Tuesday morning they were in the basement office in the South Tower when the first plane hit. David put Sirius into his kennel and went to check what was happening and what he could do to help. As he left the office, David said to his partner, "I'll be back for you."

David, along with six firemen and an injured woman, got trapped by debris in one of the tower's lower floors. It took nearly five hours for them to be found and rescued. Thankfully, they all survived. But it was too late for Sirius. He had perished when the towers fell. It took nearly four months to find his remains. When they were discovered, he was still in his kennel. On January 22, 2002 a still heart-broken David kept the promise he'd made to his partner. He carried his beloved Sirius's body, which was draped in the American Flag, out of his tomb and into the daylight. K-9 Sirius was given a police hero's farewell complete with bagpipes and a twenty-one-gun salute. It was a tribute he deserved. His memorial service was attended by 400 people, of which one hundred were from K-9 units across the country. At the end of the service, Sirius's metal dish, which was found in the rubble near his body, was presented to David Lim. Sirius's name may not be on the memorial, but it has been inscribed upon the hearts of all who knew and loved him.

Sometimes, heroes have four paws.

In addition, there is another group of heroes whose names are not on the wall. They are 9/11 responders and citizens who, although were not killed on 9/11, are dying from the effects of that day. Those responders acted with the same courage, grace, and selflessness as their deceased counterparts. Their lives have been forever changed by the toxic remnants of the attack. The various cancers and lung problems they are suffering with are stealing their lives, their quality of life, day-by-day. They, along with the innocent citizens on the street, (who are also suffering from the aftermath of debris and toxic elements released into the air), deserve to be honored and remembered as much as those ones who did not make it out alive.

In the ensuing years since that terrible morning, the American people have adjusted. Some have learned not to take our freedoms for granted; others still have a way to go. Unfortunately, there is still a lack of equality… the breeding ground for the anger and hatred that has caused so much tragedy throughout history. There is still too much hatred and not enough love and kindness. Too much division and not enough cooperation.

The healthy, human heart looks the same in any body. Neither color, creed, country-of-origin, nor sexual orientation change its anatomical make-up or its physiological function. As much as many may rail against the knowledge, we are more alike than different and have more in common than not. We all love, laugh, grieve, fear, get angry. But it is how we respond to and act upon those emotions that separate the humane from the inhumane.

We still may have differences, but they should not make us enemies. They should be used to educate, expand, and enhance our knowledge of the human race. Help give a better understanding so that no matter what, we know that we are all citizens of this world. Together, as people, we can help all humankind. By remembering to behave in ways that honor the sacrifices made by so many throughout history so that all can have the freedoms we enjoy, and not take those freedoms for granted, is one way. And, to continue to behave in ways that enhance this world and not become like the terrorists who wish to destroy it is another.

Sadly, there will always be fanatics that will use any excuse to further their "cause." Those who will gladly destroy something, anything, just because it doesn't fit in with their radical beliefs. Unfortunately, it is very difficult to defend against these people—who may be our neighbors or co-workers—because their fanaticism comes first. Friendship may not always work, but if we try and remember to treat others the way we wish to be treated then, hopefully, it will go a long way in reducing some of the hatred and tension that causes so much heartbreak.

If 9/11 taught us anything, is that our well-intentioned actions may not always be received in the way we had intended. What good we do for one, may anger another. However, that should not stop us from doing what we have done for the last century or so, using are resources to help others. We can't be responsible for how others interpret or misinterpret are actions. We need to keep going, keep doing the most good for the most people.

I think we have also become more aware. Not just for security and safety, but also to the needs of our fellow humans. Whether it be national—enacting laws that make things more equitable—or local neighbor helping neighbor, or stranger helping stranger, I think we've become more conscientious and compassionate, lending a helping hand when needed.

We are a great country. We help to make justice, liberty, and freedom more than simply words, but to also put them into action, make them real for all people, not just the privileged few. We must continue to behave in ways that uplift humanity, to learn respect for all, educate ourselves so we can understand others' points of view, because suspicion is usually based more on fear than on facts. Actions trigger reactions. Ignorance breeds intolerance. Intolerance breeds hatred. Hatred breeds anger and anger can breed unthinkable acts of violence. Just as conversely, tolerance breeds trust. Trust breeds understanding. Understanding breeds respect. Respect breeds love. Humans, unlike most other species, have been designed so that we can love any other human. We are not restricted by the territorial-like behaviors that constitute the actions of so many other species. In learning from our mistakes, we can move forward in positive ways so we can be proud to say we are not only citizens of the United States of America, but citizens of this world.

We are all in this together, all on the same planet together. Let us hope that never again should we have to ask: Why? Who? How? What happened?

WHY?

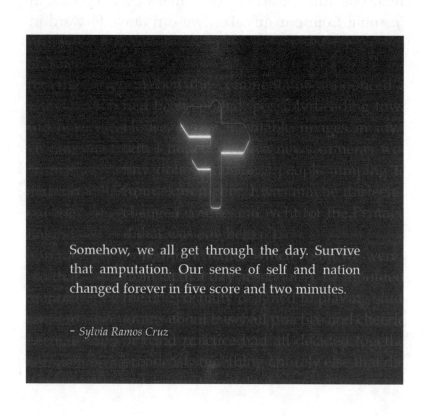

Somehow, we all get through the day. Survive that amputation. Our sense of self and nation changed forever in five score and two minutes.

– *Sylvia Ramos Cruz*

Where To?

Sylvia Ramos Cruz

I

"As to America, I say to it and its people a few words: I swear to God that America will not live in peace before peace reigns in Palestine, and before all the army of infidels depart the land of Muhammad, peace be upon him."

New York Times, Monday, October 8, 2001,
translated text of Osama bin Laden broadcast

Eighteen years later we're still cursed by those words. Hear daily about war in Afghanistan, the Taliban, terrorism, atrocities world-wide linked directly to that day. Face consequences that stretch *ad infinitum* like the plume of black and purple fumes rising from the hole in the side of the first tower. First responders dying from working day after day in the molten ossuary of the World Trade Center. Crumbling liberties at home....

And, still, no peace in Palestine.

I know it well
the boom of planes high in the sky

all night 9/11 into 9/12
fighter jets keep us awake

spirits dropping from the sky—
no way to unremember

seraphim revealed
through fire smoke embers ashes

ashes ashes
we all fall down

II

*Praise the great windows where immigrants from the kitchen
could squint and almost see their world, hear the chant of nations...*

Alabanza: In Praise of Local 100 - Martín Espada

February 1990. Just before I move to New Mexico, my sister and I celebrate her birthday. Brunch at Windows on the World. 1,284 feet into the heavens. Slowly, I approach the floor-to-ceiling windows. *¡Imaginate. Alguien limpia estas ventanas. Por fuera!* See my reflection suspended in the ether. Feel the building sway. (Or do I?) Look through chiffon clouds at cars like specks on the ground. Hudson waters shimmer frigid and grey. Lady Liberty, torch aloft, beckons me. I didn't come through Ellis Island. Technically, am not an immigrant. Yet I crossed an ocean from Puerto Rico to New York to call this place home.

I remember well the silvery metal posts between glass panes. Gold-papered walls. Tiered table spaces. White tablecloths. So far from the island where I was born. Far even from the south Bronx where I grew up. Remember nothing of the meal and, worse, nothing of the wait-staff. Wonder how many of those souls celebrated by Espada worked there then.

for workers
who perished that fiery day

107

for those
who were absent that morning

for those
who managed to escape

for those
who put their lives on the line

for those
who died that others may live

for those
who persevere though scarred

for those
who despair and those who hope

for those
who keep their lost ones in mind

for those
who live in loved ones' hearts

for those
who work each day for Peace

¡Alabanza!

III

"Since September 11, an entire generation of young Americans has gained new understanding of the value of freedom, and its cost in duty and in sacrifice."

New York Times, Monday, October 8, 2001
President George W. Bush

9/11/01. Americans huddle around TVs from 8:46 a.m. 'til far into the night. At the office I turn a blind eye as staff sneak into the breakroom to catch snippets of the Twin Towers exhale crimson fire and black smoke. Rain doom on a dumbfounded city. Disappear from Big Apple's skyline. Forever.

For the first and only time
in my life as a physician and surgeon
I resent having to attend to my patients.
I want to stop

Bear witness to this
incomprehensible event.
Mourn
as a mortally wounded colossus in my city
falls to its knees,
collapses into itself.
Stop

Think of my family and friends—
New Yorkers dyed-in-the-wool.
Are they safe?
How are they
coping with this calamity?
Stop

How will I?

Somehow, we all get through the day. Survive that amputation. Our sense of self and nation changed forever in five score and two minutes.

I remember my trip to Big Bend National Park three weeks later. Looking surreptitiously and suspiciously at all "middle-eastern looking" men. (almost fifty percent of the men there!) Asking *muchachos* on the other side of the river, *¿Cuanto?*, for a ride in their wooden pontoon across the narrow, shallow Rio Grande. Sitting down in midday heat for a *taco* and beer in Boquillas, Mexico. Carefree crossing shut from 2002 to 2013. Cross-border tourism, town's lifeblood, drained. Official port of entry now boasts a ferry and passport control center. I imagine those young *empresarios Mexicanos* are gone. Perhaps *cruzaron la frontera del norte* to find work.

IV

"This award is not just for me. It is for those forgotten children who want education. It is for those frightened children who want peace. It is for those voiceless children who want change."

Malala Yousafzai, *seventeen-year-old Pakistani activist on winning the Nobel Peace Prize in 2014*

Easy to stay mired in this post-9/11 miasma. Hard to see a world without constant surveillance. TSA lines. Drone executions. Muslim bans. *Niños* crying in cages at the border. People chanting "Send her back" (to where she came from, though she comes from here). A world without endless war. Without the terror of the "war on terror."

But life is built on visions not of what is but what can be. Like women in 1848 envisioning woman's suffrage. Winning it in 1920. Like Helen Keller, unable to hear or see, delivering her message of respect for human rights to millions around the globe. Like earth-bound humans walking on the moon in '69. Like Nelson Mandela fighting to end a seventy-four-year-old brutal regime of white supremacy and apartheid. Then, reminding us, "It always seems impossible until it's done." Like eighty-nine-year-old Dolores Huerta still advocating for workers, women, children. Organizing and teaching students to become community leaders working for social justice. Like sixteen-year-old Greta Thunberg, autistic schoolgirl, standing alone outside the Swedish Parliament, week after week. Asking politicians to act posthaste on climate change. Like disparate people coming together to bring California condors, Ice Age birds, back from the edge of extinction. Watching them ride thermal waves high above the jagged edges of Big Sur.

white-banded
black, finger-tipped wings touch horizons
fly free

Glossary

¡Imaginate. Alguien limpia estas ventanas. Por fuera!
    Imagine! Someone cleans these windows. On the outside!
Alabanza: Praise
muchachos: young men
Cuanto: how much
empresarios Mexicanos: Mexican entrepreneurs
cruzaron la frontera del norte : crossed the northern border
niños: children

War is its own kind of hell. Some people cannot truly understand what our children, our friends, our colleagues, our first responders, and our soldiers go through to protect our freedom and how 9/11 affected so many lives.

—Marilyn L. Pettes Hill

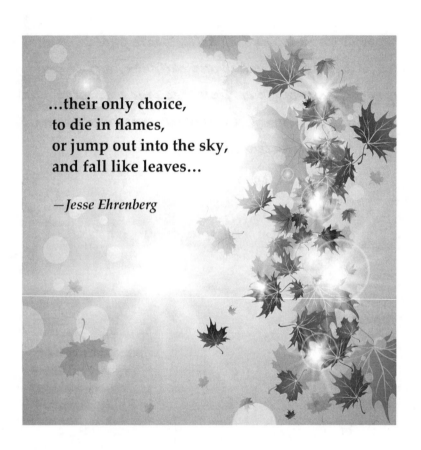

...their only choice,
to die in flames,
or jump out into the sky,
and fall like leaves...

—Jesse Ehrenberg

9/11

Jesse Ehrenberg

1

I remember watching the
planes on television
as they hit the buildings,
first one,
  then another,
crashing through steel and glass,
exploding into flame and smoke.
And the people
trapped,
more than
one hundred stories
above the ground,
their only choice,
to die in flames,
or jump out into the sky,
and fall like leaves
screaming
(screams that would
never be heard,
but our imaginations
would never forget).

2

And then the towers
collapsing into themselves,
first one,
   then the other,
in a kind of
strangely graceful
symmetry,
a ballet
of terror and death,
leaving us in a world
obscured
in clouds of
dust and debris,
staring,
trying to make sense.

3

Now,
so many years later,
we look back,
and see
that the tragedy
that once
brought us together,
has now
torn us apart,
and we've become
a nation of strangers,

cowering
behind walls,
afraid of our neighbors,
and watching
as America slowly dies
bleeding
her freedoms away;
first one,
    then another,
until empty of ideals,
our country
collapses in on itself,
leaving us
standing in the ruins,
trying to make sense.

A brilliant blue sky above a typical New Mexico adobe-style home. "Home" takes many forms. On September 11, 2001, "home" was all of the United States.

Away from Home

We were stranded in paradise.

—Cornelia Gamlem

It was hot...late-summer-desert-it-can-kill-you hot. The engine's purring offered assurance I would soon be with Walter.

— *Patricia Walkow*

Is that her? As the car got closer, I could see inside. My heart was beating faster.

— *Walter Walkow*

Apart

Patricia Walkow and Walter Walkow

Tuesday, September 11, 2001

__H__er story, Los Angeles: I had just awakened and followed my normal business trip routine of turning the television on before getting out of bed in my hotel room. That week I had flown to Los Angeles to visit with a client. As the image filled the TV screen, I saw the World Trade Center buildings collapse and the image repeated several times. I had lived in the Los Angeles area for eleven years prior to moving to a community near Albuquerque, New Mexico. During my years in L.A., I was frequently confronted with filming venues...fire engines racing to a fire that wasn't real, and police cars apprehending criminals who were just acting. The images on the screen before me seemed to be just another movie.

Which idiots would make a movie like this? Why would they give someone such a diabolical idea?

Disgusted at yet another example of Hollywood excess, I went into the bathroom of my hotel room to take my shower.

Exiting the bathroom, I couldn't believe the same movie was still showing. I changed the channel. More of the same.

Oh no!

Hollywood writers didn't conjure up this one. It was too bizarre.

Stunned into near-disbelief and fueled by anger, I listened to the radio in my rental car as I drove to my office, about thirty minutes from the hotel. Incongruously, I thought of Bugs Bunny, who would sometimes comment on a prickly situation with another cartoon character by using the phase, "Of course, this means war."

During my drive, it dawned on me my sister-in-law worked at the World Trade Center.

Oh my God! Jeanne works right there. I have to contact Alex!

As soon as I got to my desk, I called my brother in New York.

"All circuits are busy," was the message I heard.

I dialed again. "All circuits are busy." And again. "All circuits are busy." I tried my cell phone. The line went dead.

Next, I called my husband, Walter, at our house in Corrales, New Mexico. "All circuits are busy." Then, I tried contacting him at his office. "All circuits are busy."

Alone in my cubicle, I took a deep breath, and just sat there: numb, then pissed, then apprehensive as to what, if anything, would come next.

The newsfeed available through my computer told me all the planes nation-wide had been grounded. They wouldn't be in the air until the following week. At least I had a rental from Hertz which I picked up the previous night. There were also trains and buses between Los Angeles and Albuquerque.

My mind started to create not-completely-rational scenarios: *Suppose there's no fuel...I have feet...Could I manage to walk east, across the Mohave desert? How long would it take me? How much water would I have to carry? I need the right shoes...I should buy a pair of walking shoes tonight. Would Walter ride his horse into Arizona, bring another horse along, and meet me somewhere in the middle of the state? What a story...What romance...Suppose we'll be separated for months?*

By now I was mentally exhausted, and had been at my client's site over two hours. It wasn't going to be a productive week. I tried to concentrate on my work, and made some headway on one of my projects, but it was evident I would not be able to charge them for all the hours my body was there, because my mind was definitely elsewhere.

At lunch, I called my husband at home and he answered. We agreed to keep in touch every few hours by land line, cell phone, or email...any method that would work.

Then I dialed Alex in New York again, and when he answered, I knew immediately he had not yet heard from Jeanne. I spent just a few minutes with him on the phone, to release the line in case his wife called.

Meanwhile, I started to think how I would get home. The rest of the day crawled along, and when I called my brother again, I was relieved to hear Jeanne, though covered in debris, had made it home from lower Manhattan. I could only imagine what she had witnessed, and how frightened Alex must have been.

His story, Albuquerque: It was close to 9 a.m. and I was driving to work at Sandia National Labs, located on Kirtland Air Force Base, which is adjacent to Albuquerque's airport. The runways are shared, making it a joint civilian-military airport. I was almost at the entrance gate when I noticed stopped cars ahead of me. This was unusual because Kirtland is an open base—anyone can enter. *What's going on?*

As I approached the gate, I saw a guard performing identification checks. I produced my badge. He looked at it, then at me, handed it back, and waved me on. *Must be something going on, maybe an exercise.* I immediately noticed the sky was quiet. At that time of the morning, there were always commercial aircraft landings and takeoffs. I continued to my office, totally unaware of what had happened. Usually, I do not listen to the radio while I drive to work, preferring to listen to some music CDs. That morning was no different, though I did briefly hear about a plane crash in Pennsylvania when I first turned on the radio for a momentary traffic report.

As soon as I got inside my building, people were walking around very excited. I stopped one of my co-workers and asked, "What's going on?"

"Don't you know?"

"Know what?" I said.

"About the planes that hit the World Trade Center and the Pentagon. Go check the internet!"

Within twenty minutes, I became aware of the extent of the destruction and the fact that all flights were grounded. That explained the lack of air traffic.

My boss made his way toward our area and announced the base was going on high alert, and we all had to leave. He had no idea when we would be allowed to return and a number of us had been designated as "mission essential," meaning we could be called back at any time.

We exited the building and left the base. By then, the airport had come alive with military activity. We saw and heard fighter jets—F-16s—fill the sky. Within hours of the terrorist attacks, the Air National Guard's 150th Fighter Wing (called the "Flying Tacos") were flying patrols over key resources in the western United States and continued to do so for several months.

I realized my wife, Pat, was stranded in L.A. on a business trip. *I wonder if she knows? Is she safe? Will there be other attacks? Where? We need to be together. But how will she get home?*

Several transportation options came to mind: Amtrak railroad, Greyhound bus, car—she did have a rental car. Driving would be the last option, since it would mean she would have to drive alone through the Mohave Desert. At that time of the year, it is really, really hot, and it's also about a 900-mile trip from LA to Albuquerque. An overnight stop would be necessary.

When I get Pat on the phone, I'll push the other options first. While I assumed she was not in any immediate danger, there was still the possibility of more attacks.

We need to be together...and soon.

My attempts to reach her were not successful, at first. But we finally connected by phone when I got home. It was a relief to hear her voice, but that was quickly replaced by my anxiousness about how and when she would return to Albuquerque. I proposed the transportation options I thought she should pursue and strongly suggested driving should be the last resort.

She listened, but was non-committal, reminding me more than once that she had a rental car, and it might be the best option for getting home.

Wednesday and Thursday, September 12 and 13

Her story, Los Angeles: Walter asked me not to drive from Los Angeles to Albuquerque. I would be alone across one of the most desolate, yet hauntingly beautiful landscapes...the Mohave Desert. Although I didn't agree with his request, I acquiesced, and pursued other transportation options.

I called Amtrak...impossible to get through to them. Was it because people who didn't have a car were trying to make reservations? Their website displayed the train schedule between Union Station in Los Angeles and Albuquerque. When I attempted to make a reservation, the system crashed. After two more scheduling attempts failed, I gave up on Amtrak.

Hell, I had a car. Yet, there was Walter's request....

Greyhound...I would try Greyhound. The itinerary for the trip between Los Angeles and Albuquerque involved about twenty-two travel hours and a bus change. I was afraid to call them...afraid I *would* get through because I have never liked bus travel. But I called.

On hold for about thirty minutes, I hung up.

Again, I tried. I never could get through to a human being. I don't remember using their website...I really don't like bus travel.

And hell, I had a car.

I tallied the hours I had actually accomplished any work since arriving at my client's site. In a day-and-a-half, I worked exactly four hours and twenty-two minutes.

My mind made up, I would let Walter know later in the day that I planned to drive home and would stay overnight in Arizona.

All this aggravation of finding alternate transportation wasn't necessary. The drop-off charge for retuning the rental car would be steep, I knew, but it was an extraordinary circumstance. Getting home was the most important consideration.

But I needed to tell Hertz, wondering how many hours I'd be on the phone trying to reach them.

As I logged in to my Hertz account, a message popped up. I don't remember the exact wording, but it was something like:

Dear Hertz Customer:

If you picked up a rental vehicle prior to 8 a.m. on the West Coast on September 11, 2001, you may return the car to any location within the U.S. or Canada. We are waiving the drop-off fee. Please drive carefully and get home safely to your family.

Hertz's approach to the problem seemed very kind, very humane. I emailed Hertz my contract number, told them I would drop the car off at The Albuquerque Sunport on September 14 or 15 (I gave myself another day, just in case I needed it), and thanked them for their generosity. Then I added, "I will be your customer for life."

The rest of the day was a blur, and when I left the office that Wednesday evening, I went shopping for a pillow, a blanket, two gallons of water, a pair of sneakers, a flashlight, some flares, and some snacks. My plan was to leave Los Angeles around noon on Thursday and travel as far as Flagstaff, Arizona, where I would stay overnight. I called Walter.

"I'll meet you in Flagstaff," he said.

"Walt, that isn't necessary. I already told Hertz I would return the car to Albuquerque."

"OK, then I'll meet you at the Owl Café on Friday, the 14th, at noon."

The Owl Café is an Albuquerque restaurant near the freeway.

"OK," I said.

The following day, Thursday, at around 12:30 p.m., I bid farewell to everyone at the office and headed east. At Barstow, my trip across the desert started in earnest, and the afternoon sun threw long shadows, making the scrubby, bare mountains glow. I felt protective of the landscape. *Hey, you terrorist lunatics, this is my country. Keep your murderous, filthy hands off it.*

I mentally noted each highway call box I passed, and their existence made me feel I was not isolated from the rest of the world. On my cell phone, I called my husband or one of my sisters every hour...that was their request. At 9 p.m. I pulled into the hotel in Flagstaff, had a bite to eat at a nearby restaurant, and went to bed. But it was impossible to sleep well.

His Story, Corrales, NM: The base was completely sealed. I could not go to work, but since I was on the "Essential Personnel List," I was required to stay in communication by e-mail with my boss...just in case. At home, the TV was on almost all the time, and I heard the number of casualties grow by the hour. It was very hard to keep my eyes dry.

I thought of my mother. *Does she know? She must. What is she thinking?* I called her.

"Hi Mom, how are you?"

"Oh hi, Walter, I'm alright." (I never heard her say that she is not alright!).

"Mom, have you heard about the attacks on the World Trade Center and Pentagon?"

There was a pause in her voice. Finally, she said, "You know, this is the first time since we came to America that I do not feel safe."

At first, I did not comprehend what she meant, but after about a minute it made sense. She lived in Germany during World War II, survived the bombings and food shortages, then came to America with my father, my brother, and me, to be safe, to start a new life.

"I know, Mom; it doesn't seem we're as safe as we once were. There's something terrible happening in the world today and now we are part of it. None of the world is safe anymore."

I asked how she was managing with the fall leaves (After my father died, she lived by herself on a few acres in New Jersey's Pine Barrens). She complained about the constant raking. We made some more small talk and then I hung up. It disturbed me that she did not feel safe. It took a lot for her to make that statement. But this event was "a lot."

The rest of the afternoon I spent talking with Pat about her travel plans. That night I tried to stay busy and not watch too much TV. At least I had my dog, Cheyenne, as company. I believe dogs know when we are sad and upset. That evening Cheyenne was very clingy. He knew.

I was notified the base was now unsealed, but only to authorized personnel, and that included me. Thursday at the base was tense. The guards seemed especially vigilant and the mood in the office was somber. There were outbursts of anger, and it was hard to concentrate on anything. Most of us left early.

Pat called in the morning to say she was leaving L.A., and while she was in the early hours of her trip, she called me a few times. I was concerned she was alone and I was anxious to see her on Friday.

Friday, September 14

Her story, Eastbound I-40, Arizona to New Mexico: It's so beautiful...Monument Valley to my left...Painted Desert to my right...this is my country. I emphasized the word "country" and started to cry. It was grief, but mostly anger.

Shaking, I pulled to the shoulder and kept the engine running. It was hot...late-summer-desert-it-can-kill-you hot. The engine's purring offered assurance I would soon be with Walter. Finally, I calmed down, and watched some traffic pass. I listened to the President's speech at the National Cathedral in Washington, D.C., during a service to help the nation—a nation in mourning, a nation furious. President George W. Bush was never an eloquent speaker, but on this day, his words were perfect.

About 12:30 p.m., I pulled off the exit ramp and noticed Walter pacing in the restaurant parking lot. Usually late for things, this time he was early and glancing at the eastbound highway lanes. He checked his watch. *I need to stop for gas. Did I tell him the car is dark blue?*

His Story, Albuquerque: It was Friday morning and I was impatient. I wanted to be sure Pat was OK. I dropped Cheyenne at doggy day dare before going to work. Pat called mid-morning and told me she'd be in Albuquerque by lunch time. We'd see each other in a few hours.

I was in the parking lot of the Owl Café at noon, where I could see the traffic exiting I-40 onto Eubank Blvd. A few minutes passed. *Where is she? Suppose something happened?* I didn't notice she had pulled into a gas station adjacent to the restaurant. Finally, I saw the Ford Taurus with California plates pull into the parking lot. *Is that her?* As the car got closer, I could see inside. My heart was beating faster. I got to the driver's door just as she was getting out. Relieved, I was shaking and just hugged her. I continued to hold on to her and didn't know what to say.

But I knew now that we were together, we could cope with September 11, 2001.

We marveled at the people who risked their lives to search through the rubble and dust.

— *Joyce Hertzoff*

Always on My Mind

Joyce Hertzoff

My husband and I woke on 9/11/01 in our daughter's condo, ate a leisurely breakfast, and turned on the TV while we took turns using the bathroom. The night before we'd watched a show on BBC America, but that morning on that station, newscasters chatted in tony British accents about terrorism and terrorists as abstract concepts. We had no idea why, until we changed the channel to a New York station in time to catch a replay of early footage of a plane hitting one of the World Trade Center buildings. Then the second one was hit and the two towers slowly imploded and fell like my heart was doing. That image was immediately seared into my brain. I blinked, hoping it was a movie.

What was going on?

The buildings that marked the southern tip of Manhattan were gone. They'd been clearly visible from the George Washington Bridge as we crossed it the day before on our drive through the city to visit our daughter in Mamaroneck, northeast of New York City. We'd visited both buildings in the years when my husband worked in lower Manhattan. Now they were no more.

We'd driven from Columbus, Ohio, where we lived at the time, for birthday celebrations for me on the twelfth and our daughter on the sixteenth.

Instead of a fun time, the feeling of sadness permeated the week.

Empty cars, left at the Mamaroneck and Larchmont stations by folks who worked at the World Trade Center, were constant reminders of what happened. We watched the reports about the plane crashing into the Pentagon and the one that crashed in Pennsylvania. That only added to the pervasive grief.

In every restaurant we visited in the next few days, people were on phones with friends and relatives, asking whether they heard from a brother or sister, some crying as they called one person after another. We passed at least three memorial services every day, and that was just in Westchester. We couldn't avoid being caught up in the sorrow.

Firemen and other first responders from Westchester fire houses as well as city firemen who lived in the county spent much of their time helping at the site. The enormity of the effort was astounding.

We were transfixed by the newscasts the entire week. We marveled at the people who risked their lives to search through the rubble and dust. Our hearts went out to those who'd lost someone, and we felt helpless, as well as frightened.

Would it happen again?

As we crossed the George Washington Bridge going west on our way back to Ohio the following weekend, I couldn't stop looking at the smoke still rising from the World Trade Center site. Driving through New Jersey, overpasses were draped with banners and flags honoring those who died.

When we arrived home in Ohio, we realized how the events touched the entire country. Emergency crews from all over our state had joined those digging through the site. A work friend was still trying to find his daughter, who worked in the buildings. We breathed a sigh of relief when he finally heard from her. She had been on her way to work when it happened.

9/11 was traumatic for our country. At least for a while, we were united. I hope that it won't take another disaster like it to bring us together again.

My luggage—but not my husband's—
missed the connecting flight...What
else could go wrong?

—*Cornelia Gamlem*

One Happy Island

Cornelia Gamlem

The salt water felt good—soothing—I thought, emerging from my morning swim. It was the only good thing I'd experienced so far on a vacation that started out miserably. Our originating flight was delayed. My luggage—but not my husband's—missed the connecting flight. When it did arrive two days later, it took hours for the front desk to tell me it was there.

What else could go wrong?

I was hesitant about this trip from the start. We were going with my husband's work colleagues and staying in a room connected to their timeshare unit. I've never been a fan of mixing business with pleasure. My years of work experience taught me the importance of boundaries. Travelling and vacationing with co-workers provided the opportunity for learning and observing more things than you needed to know—things that could be embarrassing. It was all too close for comfort.

Everyone assured me it would be fine. "You'll be in Aruba—One Happy Island."

Happy was not an emotion I was experiencing. I'd been anxious about my lost luggage, spent too much money on clothes in the hotel gift shop, and was uneasy staying in a room on the other side of the wall from my husband's colleagues.

I wrapped a towel around me, grabbed my room key and beach shirt, and headed back inside, stopping to talk to the concierge about booking an excursion for the next day. We were interrupted by another hotel employee who walked by and simply said, "A plane just crashed into the World Trade Center."

The concierge and I had already established we were both native New Yorkers. With no further details, we assumed it was a small, private plane. "They can be so dangerous in crowded airspace," I said. "Can you imagine the mess in lower Manhattan?" I booked the excursion and headed to my room. My husband would be back from his dive excursion in an hour. Plenty of time to shower and change.

When I entered my room, for some unconscious reason I turned on the TV before heading to the shower. CNN was announcing another plane had made its attack on the World Trade Center's second tower. *Oh shit.* I realized in that moment these were jet planes and this was not an accident. The image of fire and oily, black smoke dominated the TV screen. The towel around me was coming loose. I pulled it off, let it drop to the floor, and sunk down into the nearby upholstered chair— damp bathing suit be damned.

The images on the TV changed. Now I was looking at a shocked President Bush, who for an instant seemed paralyzed. Next, was a defiant New York Mayor Rudy Giuliani. My hometown—the place where I was born and raised—was under attack, and lower Manhattan was more than a mess. It was mayhem. A war zone. *Was my family in New York okay?*

Watching the images replay on the TV, I felt I was being pulled into a hypnotic trance. It was all too surreal. Was I losing track of time or was time standing still? Then the next horrific report came—a third plane hit the Pentagon in Arlington, Virginia. My son lived and worked in Arlington. He would later report that from his office they could see the smoke from the Pentagon.

Debilitated, I sunk deeper into the chair. This had to be a bad dream, a nightmare, just like this late-summer escape. At that moment, the sound of the door opening jarred me back to reality. My husband came bounding into the room announcing how great the morning dive had been.

"The United States is under attack," I told him. "Two jets were hijacked and flew into The World Trade Center. A third into the Pentagon."

A puzzled look came over his face. "You're kidding."

"Would I joke about something like this?" I shouted, startled at his reaction. He had, after all, served four years in the Marines. Then it hit me. He's processing this horrendous news. And President Bush wasn't paralyzed. He was processing.

At that moment, more breaking news was reported. A fourth jetliner had crashed near Shanksville, Pennsylvania.

It was not until that evening our son called, and we got news from home. He confirmed what we suspected. The area around the nation's capital was in chaos that morning: traffic snarled like never before, the Metro public transportation line at a standstill, and phone lines and cell towers overloaded. A police state was declared for the city of Washington, D.C. Everyone with us on this trip lived in Northern Virginia, about twenty miles from the Pentagon. Everyone was concerned about families and loved ones. One couple brought their twelve-year-old niece, and they couldn't get through to her family for days.

Our son shared more news. He had called my parents, who lived on Long Island, to check on them. He learned they were supposed to fly to Pittsburgh that morning to visit my sister. They were waiting for a taxi to take them to LaGuardia Airport, when my brother, who lived nearby, called them with the news of the attacks. "Unpack. Flights are cancelled. You're not going anywhere." I had a moment of temporary relief. They avoided any turmoil at the airport. But wait, how far was Shanksville from Pittsburgh? Were my sister and her family okay? The places where these attacks occurred in New York, Virginia, and Pennsylvania, were all too close to where my family members lived.

There was no peace or peace of mind that week. Two days later in the elevator, a woman was visibly upset.

"Her brother works in the Trade Center, and she hasn't had any news—can't get through to her family," her husband explained.

I'd been to the World Trade Center, once, for a business meeting. On that trip, as I rode the high-speed elevator to the top floor, I was amused at the trepidation in the eyes of some colleagues who'd never experienced a ride to the top of a skyscraper. Now, on a beautiful tropical island, I was empathizing with the fear in this

140

stranger's eyes.

I later learned that my sister-in-law saw one of the jets fly into the World Trade Center as she was driving to work on the Grand Central Parkway in Queens, New York. She was surprised there weren't more accidents on the roads that day. Their neighbors lost two family members, both of whom worked for Cantor Fitzgerald, the financial services firm that lost two thirds of its New York workforce that day. And my nephew—her son—was a volunteer firefighter. His station worked at Ground Zero in the aftermath.

On the beach in Aruba we met other Americans— from New York, D.C., and elsewhere. This brought us some solace and feeling of unity, but we couldn't escape the anxiety, the feeling of being cut off. Smartphones and tablets weren't yet part of our everyday lives. There was another complicating factor. Aruba's government controlled the island country's telecommunications. It was difficult and expensive to make calls to the outside world. With air traffic suspended, there was collective uncertainty about when and how we'd get home.

"Not a bad place to be stranded," people would say to us later. On the contrary, it was. I just wanted nothing more than to be home even if fighter jets were eerily patrolling the empty skies over the nation's capital.

Some air traffic began to resume on Thursday, but it was limited. Our situation presented a unique dilemma. We flew on United Airlines using frequent flyer miles, but United only had one round trip flight per week, every Saturday, between Virginia and Aruba. My husband spent a frustrating Wednesday morning on the phone with them only to learn our scheduled flight for Saturday, September 15 was cancelled. Find another way home. My heart sank.

We were stranded in paradise.

Rather than call another airline and be placed on an endless hold, we went to the local airport that afternoon. We wanted to talk to someone in person. American Airlines could get us on a direct flight, but not until next Wednesday. I could feel my stomach churn, my fists clench. Great. Another week before I see my home, hug my son, sleep in my own bed. I watched as my husband offered the agent his credit card in exchange for tickets home, wishing it brought some relief. It didn't.

Time moved slowly over the next seven days. We waited and watched. We watched the others in our group leave on their scheduled flights on Saturday. We watched other Americans leave day by day. We watched as new vacationers—none of them from the United States—arrived, adding to the isolation we felt. At any other time and under different circumstances, I would have relished meeting people from different countries and cultures. Instead, I was feeling uneasy, unreasonable resentment toward them. How dare they be here enjoying themselves?

Wednesday, September 19, couldn't arrive fast enough. Our direct flight from Aruba to Washington Dulles was scheduled to arrive at approximately 10:30 p.m. As we boarded, I could sense the tension among the passengers and crew members who had, after all, lost colleagues. I felt a wave of relief as we took off. I couldn't get off this happy island fast enough.

The mood on the flight was somber. I caught myself thinking, "Can't they fly this plane any faster?" Irrational, I know. I just wanted to get home.

We touched down at Dulles about thirty minutes early and the passengers let out a collective cheer. Ironically, people were calm and courteous deplaning—unlike the usual scurrying to get carryon items down from the overhead bins, rush toward the door and off the plane. Now, everyone took their time, and they stopped to thank every crew member they could for getting us home safely. As we exited the plane, other flight attendants holding American flags greeted us.

While my husband made his way to claim the luggage, I found a pay phone—remember those? I called my son. "We're on the ground. We're safe. We'll be at our house in thirty minutes." As I hung up, I felt my legs weaken. I caught myself before I fell to my knees, but thought I could kiss the ground.

I'm home.

In the midst of chaos and uncertainty, there's truly no place like home.

— *Loretta Hall*

There's No Place Like Home

Loretta Hall

I was beginning to feel like a real author. Unlike the two books I had written as works for hire, I now had a contract to write about a topic of my own choosing. The publisher had even given me an advance, so I had been able to travel for some of my research. My topic was underground buildings, everything from Cold War nuclear refuges to modern schools, factories, and recreational facilities.

In the past three months, I had visited Phoenix, Chicago, and several cities in Ohio. Seeing subterranean structures including a university library, a shopping mall, a performing arts center, and a convention center had been exciting and energizing. I could visualize my new book developing into a stunningly-illustrated, information-filled volume.

On September 8, 2001, I flew into Minneapolis on my next research excursion. During the following two days, I explored two highway rest areas, a public library, a university laboratory building, a university book store and administration building, and two visitor centers at historic sites—all built into the earth. My trip was a huge success, providing valuable experiences and photographs.

September 11th got off to a pleasant start. Even my alarm clock sounded cheery. I was anticipating an interview later that morning with an architect who had designed several famous underground buildings, including a couple I had seen the day before.

I turned on the television as I started my morning routine. What I saw was *not* routine. A commercial airliner had crashed into one of the Twin Towers in New York City. In contrast with my current interest in underground buildings, I had previously written some reference book chapters about skyscrapers. I knew that a sizeable airplane had hit the Empire State Building decades before. I also knew that the design of the World Trade Center towers had specifically taken into account the possibility of an aviation accident and the buildings were designed to withstand such an impact. As awful as the destruction was, I knew the building would continue to stand.

Feeling sad about the tragic incident, I stepped into the shower. After I had gotten dressed and dried my hair, I stepped back into the living area of my hotel room. As I looked back at the television, I was horrified to watch a second airliner fly directly into the second tower. I was stunned. There was no way this could be an accident. The first crash, yes. That was my natural assumption. But this second impact, no way.

I stood, mesmerized, in front of the TV set for a few moments. Then my brain started working again. What should I do? I needed to leave in a few minutes for my interview. What was the proper way to handle that? Should I call and cancel it? Should I go ahead and show up as scheduled? What is the protocol for conducting normal business in the midst of a terrorist attack?

Ten minutes later, I found my rental car in the parking lot and headed for my interviewee's office. From the radio, I heard the unthinkable news: one of the towers had collapsed. I didn't understand it. I couldn't comprehend what was happening.

As I drove, I started thinking about my family. My husband was a civil engineer—a logical, pragmatic person. He had gotten home from his business trip on Saturday, and he would be fine. My eldest daughter was staying with relatives in Ohio, so I knew she would have emotional support. My middle daughter and her husband had each other to rely on. But my youngest daughter was away from family, living in her college dorm in North Carolina. I needed to call her.

I pulled into the parking lot at my destination, turned off the car, and got out my cell phone. My college student daughter and I had a long talk about what was happening. I knew our conversation had been reassuring to her, and it helped me to connect with family too. I would call my husband and our other daughters later.

The architect was in his office, and he invited me in. We exchanged a few awkward comments about the strangeness of the situation, and then went on with our interview. Things almost seemed normal for an hour.

Back in the car, I turned on the radio again. The second tower had fallen. I wasn't surprised this time. If the first one could fall, the second one certainly could. At that time, the idea of two crumbled skyscrapers was just an abstraction. Only later would I begin to understand the devastation caused by those events.

As I drove back to my hotel, I started examining my travel plans. Should I wait until tomorrow and fly home as scheduled? Flights were being cancelled. How long might it be before I could get a plane back to Albuquerque? I decided not to take the chance.

On the way to the hotel, I happened to pass a Catholic church. I've been a Catholic all my life, and it seemed like the most natural thing to stop and go inside to pray. I parked the car, walked up to the door, and found it locked. I had grown up in a small town in Kansas and lived in Albuquerque for over twenty years. Finding a Catholic church locked on a weekday was a shock. I have since learned that this is increasingly common, especially in larger cities. But I felt cold and unfulfilled to be shut out of my place of solace.

At the hotel, I called my rental car company to see if I could just drive the car to New Mexico and return it there. No. They couldn't authorize that. I called a couple of other rental car companies. The person who answered the phone at Thrifty said that they don't usually allow that, but he happened to have a car in his lot that belonged in Texas. He said he would go ahead and let me rent it. Getting it to New Mexico would get it closer to where it should be. I could have kissed him through the phone.

I packed up my things, checked out of the hotel, and drove to the Enterprise lot to return my car. Thrifty had agreed to pick me up there. By the time I finished the paperwork and got into my next car, it was about five o'clock in the afternoon. Now what? Should I start driving or find a motel and wait until morning? The answer was easy. I just wanted to head for home.

About eight o'clock I stopped for the night. Somewhere along the line, I bought a one-page road map of the United States so I could plan my route. I never travel now without a miniature road atlas in my luggage.

For the next two days, I drove in silence across the Midwest and Central parts of the country. Never once did I see an airplane in the sky. It was eerie.

After the longest solo drive of my life, I arrived in Albuquerque. I was tired from the emotional stress and from being on the road with only a few necessary stops for nearly 1,500 miles. I turned in my rental car, again thanking the Thrifty counterperson profusely. My husband picked me up and took me home. Being back in my adobe-style house in the North Valley, I felt more normal than I had for several days.

In the midst of chaos and uncertainty, there's truly no place like home.

Innocent lives were lost that day, silenced then, but not forever. Their voices speak from the grave...men and women...Oh How Brave.

— *Paul D. Gonzales*

A Mourning in September

A poem

Paul D. Gonzales

On that day in September, I do remember when hatred appeared on the screen...Nineteen men from the Middle East, took to the skies with hate in their eyes brought death and despair to our shore...and a whole lot more. Death, surprise and fear were their mission... to bring U.S. into submission.

The cowards who flew those deadly missiles, their bodies now lay among the trash and thistles, where rats and roaches nest in their ashes.

Innocent lives were lost that day, silenced then, but not forever. Their voices speak from the grave...men and women...Oh How Brave. Innocent souls leaped to their death while exhaling their final breath. Those innocent souls paid the price and entered eternity without a wink...to accept their death, they did not shrink.

"Let's Roll" were the words those brave souls shouted... are forever etched on that precious scroll, for who doth those bells toll, of the dead, as their names are read. Their families will mourn for evermore, but happy to know we settled the score.

Our President stood upon the rubble and vowed to bring Al-Qaeda plenty of military trouble. The smoke and dust and twisted iron fell quickly under gravity's law.

Those great towers that stood erect, were felled, but we will show the world...without regret, that the U.S. will right this awful wrong and bounce back...twice as strong.

Do not despair at this happening, but keep the faith to show our strength. Those mighty towers are now re-placed with one, to show the world we have no guilt for our revenge on the cowards.

We are a nation built on freedom and free people we will stay...while men like bin Laden lie in decay. His flesh is eaten by the fish, his bones lay scattered in the ocean, his memory is nothing more than a passing no-tion.

I pray God's justice on those nineteen men as I end my prayer with a strong AMEN.

Reflections

The history of war is the history of humankind, yet we are shocked anew every time.

—Gayle Lauradunn

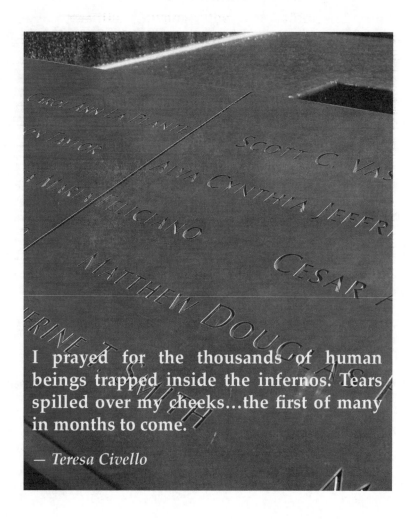

I prayed for the thousands of human beings trapped inside the infernos. Tears spilled over my cheeks...the first of many in months to come.

— *Teresa Civello*

The Home of the Brave

Teresa Civello

An Eyewitness Account of the 9/11 Attacks on New York City

1993: DRESS REHEARSAL FOR 9/11

The bomb weighed more than 1,300 pounds. Radical fundamentalists had hidden it inside a yellow Ryder van parked in the underground garage of the North Tower. The powerful device exploded on February 26, 1993, killing six civilians, including a pregnant woman, and injuring more than a thousand.

Six months later, the FBI raided a bomb factory in Queens and arrested six extremists. They planned to use chemical explosives to blow up New York City landmarks, and both the Holland and Lincoln Tunnels which funneled 200,000 vehicles each weekday from New Jersey and Pennsylvania to New York City onto the island of Manhattan. Nightmares of explosions plagued me for months.

I waited for the other shoe to drop.

SEPTEMBER 11, 2001
A Glorious Morning Explodes

Flowers in baskets hanging from every lamp post perfumed the air. I'd just come from voting in the Mayoral Primary and stood on my corner of West 14th Street and 7th Avenue. I gazed south at two familiar concrete, glass, and steel structures a mile downtown and waited for the light to change.

Then, I saw it.

A large commercial airliner swooped into Tower Two, turning the upper stories into a fireball. Vehicles traveling along 7th Avenue and 14th Street screeched to a halt. People screamed.

Then…silence. My gut told me it was no accident.

The building was ablaze. Minutes later another plane crashed into Tower One and within seconds, the building burst into flames. Black smoke unfurled from the wounded structures. Within minutes, the floral-scented air reeked with acrid smells of burning chemicals. Airborne gray dust and gritty particles soon became part of the autumn sky.

I prayed for the thousands of human beings trapped inside the infernos. Tears spilled over my cheeks…the first of many in months to come.

Blaring horns and screaming sirens shattered the silence. First responders in fire engines, police vehicles, and ambulances raced downtown in a surreal procession.

I speed-walked uptown to the 108th and Central Park assisted living facility—my client—where I resolved Medicare and Medicaid problem accounts and increased revenue. No one knew if more attacks were planned. On the way, I stopped at nearby Mount Sinai Hospital. Hundreds of people were lined up to donate blood. Later, we learned the tower victims would never arrive. I flashed my facility badge and met with the pharmacy supervisor. She agreed to provide medications for my client's residents should we run out before the city reopened key Manhattan thoroughfares.

Walking into my client's building, I discovered the lobby filled with staff, pushing each other in front of the three public pay phones. They didn't realize the lines were dead. Cell phones were equally useless. The director was in the day room, flailing his arms and rambling about bombs and death, scaring the residents. I escorted him to his private office and suggested he update the facility emergency handbook and asked the guard to keep him contained.

Since the nursing director hadn't yet arrived, I took charge and held a special staff meeting. We completed an inventory of food and medical supplies and a linen count for make-shift hammocks to ensure we could transport people from the upper floors, should Con Edison be attacked and electricity disrupted.

CBS, transmitting from the Empire State Building, was the only television station available. All the others had shifted their TV and AM-FM radio communications to the broadcast antenna atop Tower Two. Commentators speculated about more attacks. We had to keep our residents safe. The elevators were still operating, so we brought them to the first floor. The residents comforted each other as they watched the televised tragedy unfold. Many former veterans compared their wartime stories to the day's bombings. Women filled the chapel.

A third hijacked plane hit the Pentagon, killing all on board and several hundred staff. The men and women on the fourth commandeered plane had rushed the cockpit to attack the terrorists. The aircraft crashed in Pennsylvania. No one survived. Fear of more assaults overtook my feigned courage. I wept. More burning wreckage. More death.

An elderly resident put her hand over my shoulder. "Don't cry. Pray. We did that during Pearl Harbor. Americans stood together and helped any way we could. We grieved and consoled neighbors who'd lost family members on the sinking ships."

As the towers trembled, I watched in horror. Each magnificent building roared and then collapsed into itself in almost total silence. Hundreds of fire fighters and those being saved from the inferno were caught unaware as the steel girders melted. We later heard the rescuers never received a warning because their communication equipment failed. They were all now entombed under the debris.

Fierce, grayish-white plumes of smoke rose from the buckled towers. They formed raging giant dragons, racing through narrow streets, clawing after soot-covered survivors running for their lives.

During the next several hours, I struggled to create a normal routine just like any other day, except we held small support groups for our men and women who had lived through war and catastrophe. My tears continually threatened to pour out and when they did, I'd turn, wipe my face, and continue working.

We provided lunch and encouraged residents to move away from TV and sing patriotic songs. Many returned to their regular afternoon activities.

Limited telephone service had been restored. I called my elderly mother. The lines were still dead in Queens, so I dialed the local 104th precinct. I finally got through and asked the desk sergeant if he could spare a car to check on her.

"My mom's eighty-five and lives alone."

"Ma'am, we're tied up with emergencies."

"Understood. I'm working in Manhattan with the elderly. We're notifying families everyone is safe. Please ask an officer to just ring her bell and say I'm okay." Finally, he agreed.

Once we learned Con Edison was protected, I dismissed the staff who lived nearby. A skeleton crew agreed to remain overnight. Together, we provided supper and returned the residents to their apartments. The night supervisor arrived and I gave her an update.

The sun was setting when I finally left the facility at 7:00 p.m., exhausted, and worried how I would return home, five miles downtown. There were few buses on the road.

I crossed the street just as one passed. I waved my hands. Drivers are not permitted to pick up passengers anywhere other than at designated locations. But he stopped in the middle of the avenue. I stepped on to join five passengers, each seated alone at a window. One woman prayed the rosary. I reached for my money, but the driver's hand covered the fare slot.

"No one pays tonight, Miss." I thanked him and planted a grateful kiss on his bristled cheek. "Fifth Avenue is closed below 34th Street. Police and the National Guard are protecting the Empire State and Chrysler buildings."

"Fine. I can walk the mile to 14th and 7th."

I sat at the front of the bus. Exclusive Upper Eastside buildings facing Central Park flew American flags. We crossed 59th where the Plaza Hotel had placed small ones around the perimeter of its circled entrance. On both sides of Fifth Avenue, flags soared from poles hanging high from each building, forming a canopy of red, white, and blue. My throat tightened by the amazing expression of patriotism.

~~~

The City That Never Sleeps was deserted except for a few stragglers, hoping for a bus. The driver went at a slow pace, picking up every pedestrian and waiting for those running to catch a ride. A military tank blocked our movement below 34th Street. Armed soldiers entered the bus to give us the once-over and apologized for closing the southbound avenue.

We exited, and I started walking west. I must have looked worn-down. A cop sitting in a patrol car with the door opened signaled me. "Ma'am, you okay?"

"Just tired." I spotted the insignia of the 23rd Precinct on the side door. "You from the 2-3? My uncle Sal Capraro was Deputy Inspector there."

"Yeah, I remember. Where ya headed?"

"My apartment on 14th and 7th."

"Hop in."

We drove without speaking, needing the silence to regain our bearings. My corner pizzeria was still open. I hadn't eaten all day and the aroma of tomato sauce brought on acute hunger pangs.

"Wait here a couple of minutes." I dashed in the store owned by Mario and Pietro, two Italian immigrant brothers, and placed an order for two extra-large fully-loaded pies. They opened their warming oven which contained partially-baked pizza crusts waiting for toppings, along with a dozen calzones, meatball and sausage heroes wrapped in aluminum foil. I asked for all the cooked food. Fast. In less than ten minutes, everything was ready to go.

I opened my wallet, but the brothers refused the money.

"We love America. How you say it?" Mario spoke in his best English. "We give food to good people that make us safe."

He helped me carry the pies and two six-packs of cola to the patrol car. I secured the pies with the front seatbelt. "You be safe, officer."

"You, too. Thanks for the pizzas," he shouted driving off.

I re-entered the store and saw that Pietro had stacked the steaming calzones and meat heroes inside two double plastic bags. He handed over my care packages which I delivered to hungry EMTs and cops parked by St. Vincent's Hospital. Then I returned to the pizzeria for two slices. Instead, the brothers invited me to share their supper of spaghetti with oil, garlic, hot pepper flakes and grated Parmesan cheese. So much better than pizza.

Back home, I sat in front of my television, staring at continuous film of the day's horror. Hundreds of people had been trapped inside the blazing stories above the floors where the fuel-filled planes hit. Two hundred jumped from the inferno to the sidewalks below.

I finally went to bed, only to be awakened by two U.S. Air Force F-15s roaring overhead. Dozens of fighter jets had been directed by the President to fly 24/7 over New York City airspace and intercept all non-government aircraft. I was grateful for the noise.

THE AFTERMATH

On Wednesday morning, September 12th, I turned on the TV and watched the first news broadcast of a massive water rescue.

Tens of thousands of people who worked or lived south of the towers had been stranded at the edge of the Hudson River in Lower Manhattan. The Coast Guard signaled an SOS for all available boats, large and small, to evacuate civilians. Coast Guard and Merchant Marine ships, Staten Island Ferries, the Governors Island Ferry, along with hundreds of tugboats, private and commercial vessels, pleasure and fishing boats from Brooklyn, Queens, Staten Island, and New Jersey answered the call. These brave men and women formed a spontaneous flotilla of seafarers. While afraid another attack might target them, they continued to work tirelessly transporting people to safety.

The white plume, now dark gray and wider than a four-lane road, became more menacing. It sped south to the tip of Manhattan Island. With nowhere to go, the dense cloud settled on the Hudson River and required captains to employ their radar systems to dock safely at New Jersey, Brooklyn, and Long Island piers.

In nine hours, the 9/11 Boat Lift operation had evacuated more than 500,000 people, a maritime feat greater than the 300,000 Allied soldiers and sailors liberated from Dunkirk during World War II.

People on their way to work offered donuts, bagels, and coffee to police officers who arrived from every state, Canada, Mexico, and Europe in support of New Yorkers. Animal handlers with their search-and-rescue dogs also arrived that morning. First, to locate survivors. Then, to sniff out buried remains.

In our own way, my neighbors and I were like first responders. We lined the park area along the West Side Highway between Greenwich Village and Chelsea and established a rest stop for those working at the pit where the Twin Towers once stood. People brought food, beverages, sleeping bags, and blankets. Open fire hydrants dripped water sufficient for the exhausted workers to wash their soot-covered faces with donated soap and hand towels.

The resident who comforted me at my job was right—New Yorkers gave of themselves. Strangers helped strangers. Volunteers supported the men and women who remained at the smoking pyre, still digging for signs of life.

The pit, later called "Ground Zero," smoldered for one-hundred days. The air was contaminated with toxic smells and particles—burning plastics, molten metal, and asbestos. But pulverized concrete was the most dangerous. The inhaled dust caused *silicosis*, a fatal lung disease that takes several painful years to finally kill its victim. Everyone who worked or visited Lower Manhattan continued to breathe unhealthy gray dust from *every thing* and *every body*.

Smoke and grit clung to my closed windows, but still managed to creep inside my apartment. I bought several fabric masks with exhalation valves recommended by pollution experts. I wore them indoors and outside for months and still had to rinse the exposed part of my face to remove accumulated ash.

Within a few days of the attack, two brilliant spotlights replicating the Twin Towers burned every night at Ground Zero, filling the empty space and bringing us comfort.

A tall wire fence that stretched above two corners of an empty lot across from St. Vincent's Hospital, three-quarters of a mile from the Pit, was initially filled with photos of missing loved ones. A week later, thousands of condolence cards made with love by school children from across our country covered every bare piece of metal.

I had often attended government and business meetings in the towers and remember the whizzing sound of elevators racing skyward. But since their collapse, I have never returned to the site.

A memorial was erected with the names of those who perished, including 343 firemen and sixty NYPD and Port Authority police officers. But the saga of death continues. More than 2,000 first responders have since died from pulmonary disease and newly-discovered cancers.

~∿∿∿~

Several terror events have occurred in New York City since 2001. Some murdered and injured ordinary people. Others were thwarted in time.

Like so many New Yorkers who lived through that day, I developed a form of PTSD. Anxiety and uneasiness limited my freedom. I stopped traveling by subway. Eighteen years later, I still avoid all underground transportation and use slower-moving buses and taxi cabs.

Every morning I pray for the safety of our country.

And wait for the other shoe to drop.

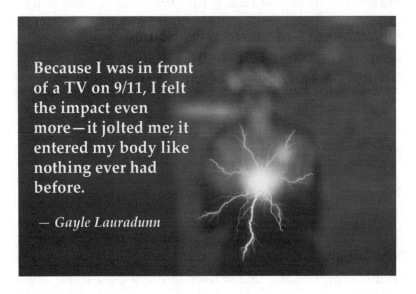

Because I was in front of a TV on 9/11, I felt the impact even more—it jolted me; it entered my body like nothing ever had before.

— *Gayle Lauradunn*

Catching a Flight

Gayle Lauradunn

Early morning fast-paced packing to get to the airport on time, I rush around the house gathering papers and notebooks I need for the meeting. The phone rings. I hesitate to answer it, but then do. It's my friend, Anna.

"Hello."

Without preamble she says, "Isn't this the day you're flying to Chicago?"

"Yes. I'm packing now. I need to leave in a few minutes so I don't miss my flight. There's so much traffic at this time of morning."

"Well, I guess you're not going now."

A puzzled pause, then I ask, "What do you mean?" Anna is highly verbal, seldom giving the listener a chance to get in a word. Her pausing, even for a moment, is unusual.

"I guess you don't have the TV on. I'll hang up and you turn it on."

In my rush to leave I had not turned on the TV. I did now, and was astounded with views of the twin towers toppling, crashing down, and people scattered everywhere. I lay down on the sofa and did not do anything for the next forty-eight hours but watch the devastation and listen to the talking heads. I had never before in my life been so glued to the TV and later could not believe the shock I experienced, nor had I ever been so engrossed by an event as to feel completely helpless. Completely numb.

The trip to Chicago was at the behest of one of the companies I worked for as a freelance marketing consultant. It was their conference and attendance was mandatory, even though the meeting content was most often worthless. The primary benefit I received from these gatherings was networking with other consultants from around the country, some of whom I met at similar meetings when we worked with the same companies.

Within a few minutes of Anna's call, I received a call from the company secretary in New York telling me everyone was being contacted as the meeting, of course, was cancelled since all airports were closed. The meeting would be rescheduled when possible. Her voice sounded shaky and I asked her if she was O.K. She said she lives on Staten Island and witnessed the attacks while riding the ferry on her way to work near Wall Street.

Over the next few days I experienced a maelstrom of mixed feelings. I was certainly relieved not to have to attend the conference, but, my goodness, at what cost? I thought about the Vietnam veterans I had worked with for seven years and wondered how they felt about this event...this horror. They had certainly been through enough horror first-hand in Vietnam.

While I was the Director of The Veterans Education Project, I had listened to their war stories multiple times.

They were preparing to talk about their experiences to high school students, and I was mentoring them as they prepared their stories so they'd be appropriate to present to the students. As a result, I was diagnosed with vicarious PTSD and suffered years of nightmares about events I had not personally witnessed.

Would today bring back the nightmares for them, for me?

The terrorist attacks continue around the world, and especially here in our own country where school children are gunned down time and again. Are our gun ownership laws strong enough? Is the NRA too powerful? What has happened to people that they think they can kill others with guns, or knives, or fire, or runaway cars?

The first attack I experienced occurred in 1970 at Kent State University. I say "experienced" meaning in the same sense I experienced the violence the veterans I worked with did. At the time I was in Florence, Italy, toting my four-month-old son around while soaking up the exquisite art and architecture. This was my first trip outside the U.S. and I was mesmerized by everything, totally lost in the history and climbing the 400 steps to the top of El Duomo to gain a view of the age-old city.

On exiting the cathedral, I was confronted by an entirely different sight: on the wall opposite were words in Italian (which I do not speak or read) to the effect of "Down with the U.S." and "All Yankees go home." These signs had not been there the day before and shocked me because I had not yet heard about the events at Kent State. Only when I returned to my friend's home in the evening did I learn what had happened. I had visited the University the year before and could not picture such an uncalled-for action occurring in that remote, peaceful environment. What had the National Guard been afraid of? What threatened them to the extent they killed innocent citizens? Innocent young people?

But are not these the same questions that apply to most violence? Fear, ignorance, greed, religion have all been major factors in the human history of violence. Because I was in front of a TV on 9/11, I felt the impact even more—it jolted me; it entered my body like nothing ever had before. I was in a war zone for the first time. But knew it would not be the last.

The history of war is the history of humankind, yet we are shocked anew every time.

...if there's one thing definitely not on the terrorist wish list, it's psychological growth.

—Colin Patrick Ennen

...it's best to describe what I *didn't* see upon leaving my dorm that day. And what I *didn't* hear. Because their absence is what stands out in my memory more than anything...

Campus was eerie, a ghost town.

—*Colin Patrick Ennen*

A Guilty Memory

Colin Patrick Ennen

The door flew inward, hitting the wall with a distinctive thud I can still hear. In its wake strode the dude from across the hall, textbook shit-eating grin on his boyish face. (A year ahead of me in Texas A&M University's Corps of Cadets, this was his privilege. The barging in, that is, not the grin. That, James Trout came by naturally.) With eyes wide like he'd just entered his first adult bookstore, he looked from me to my roommate and back then made a statement: "We're going to war."

In the movie version of my life, here's where the sound effects whiz would insert that record scratch noise. The video would rewind, and we'd watch the entrance and statement again before freezing on his ecstatic face. Sitting on your couch at home you'd cringe, possibly utter a soft "eew" as the narrator, Peter Coyote maybe, or Sam Elliot, verified the proclamation in a woeful tone. "And it would prove a nightmare," he'd add.

It's odd that Trout's bombastic assertion plays out like a recording in my mind, given the overall shoddiness of my memory. Without question it is one of the most vivid episodes stored in my organic hard drive, and of all the things I've experienced in almost forty years on Earth, from athletic achievements to natural phenomena to spicy romantic entanglements, I can recall it from that storage organ easier than almost any other. I'm *pretty* sure I hit a homerun my senior year in high school, but damn if I can remember a thing about it. And I know for a fact I saw Bob Dylan in concert once, yet the closest I've got to a memory is a general sense of blah. James Trout getting jazzed about impending war? Yep, instant, high-definition recall.

But it's a small file, just a few megabytes, ending with his evacuating our room after explaining his declaration. Like it fades out as I begin scrutinizing his position: yes, the plane crashes were unlikely to have been accidents, but, gosh, does that really mean war? And even if so, should that excite us? Whether I actually posed these questions or merely thought them, I can't remember. Considering the hierarchical structure of our relationship, I suspect the latter. (NB: The Corps of Cadets at Texas A&M University is, essentially, a military academy within the larger school. Two thousand or so students who wear uniforms to class, live in barracks, march, get inspected, etc., it is a holdover from the university's founding in the late 19th century as a land-grant college.)

Distinct as this memory is, until recently I couldn't have told you how—or even if—the scenario influenced my thinking that day. It's hard to imagine it not, though, right? First impressions matter, after all, whether they're about Timmy the plumber, a band you've never heard of, or an event that changed the course of history. They flavor things: think drinking orange juice after brushing your teeth or being told Shakespeare was the greatest playwright ever before reading a single word. Good or bad, such initial exposures direct, tint, or limit the way we think, but for the longest time I'd have told you this was not the case for the grandiose fashion in which I first learned of the 9/11 tragedy. Truth is, it was too obvious. I mean, anymore I don't really need an impetus for skepticism. But it didn't come so naturally to that twenty-year-old and required a spark. Point is, learning about the attacks in this manner may have prompted me to view succeeding events through a critical lens, to approach information intake in an analytical manner.

Also, I think a part of me was always relieved I saw no one else react as he did.

Because, other than him, that's what I've retained: reactions. Not the things happening, but how people around me responded to them. And these recollections are static. Tableaus, you might call them, or like scenes from an ancient engraving, say on a Roman triumphal arch. Only, instead of showing, I don't know, Agricola or Scipio Africanus defeating this or that barbarian tribe, it shows *the people* of Rome reacting to the news of Agricola or Scipio Africanus defeating this or that barbarian tribe.

Perhaps you note the problems here. In this metaphorical engraving, we're not just limited in what we're seeing—reaction shots as opposed to the relevant happenings—we're getting interpretations, and incomplete ones at that. The thing about a triumphal arch or, heck, Shakespeare's depiction of Richard III, England's last

Plantagenet king, is they're propaganda, just like my one-sided memories of what took place on 9/11. Except with me—insecure, way-too-hard on myself, full of regrets—it's like I've swallowed someone else's propaganda, like I got fed the barbarian side of the story or the Tudor version of the hunch-backed Richard and bought them whole hog.

The truth is, I've long harbored guilt over how I thought and behaved on that day, lamented my analysis of its events as they related to me personally. I didn't like the way I judged everybody for not being as composed and detached as I was. Of course, as with all propaganda, this guilt memory was only partly true: yeah, I acted like a damned green-blooded Vulcan, but that doesn't mean the crux of my analyses was wrong. And, like *Star Trek's* Mr. Spock, as whom I've dressed up for Halloween at least four times, my shortcomings were a function of misunderstanding emotional impact or personal connection. I still don't, to a large extent, comprehend such matters, but twenty years have allowed me to accommodate them, whereas in 2001 my world had little room. It's odd the reflection opportunity presented by this volume has, yes, forced me to confront my worldview and challenge my perspectives, but also given me leave to forgive myself for being, in fact, human.

Not that it's been an easy process.

As for this meta-analysis, it begins where this piece did, with James Trout barging into my dorm room on a Tuesday morning in early September, just as I was tying my right shoe. I don't actually feel so bad about judging him after all these years. It *was* tasteless, after all, getting giddy like he did about the prospect of war. Not surprising in the least, given his nature—small of stature, young-looking, insecure, bitter about it all—but tasteless, nonetheless. Beyond that, however, to be excited about war means to misunderstand the point of the nation's armed services, of which Trout, like me, would soon be a member. (We were Navy ROTC midshipmen, he less than a year from commissioning, me closer to 16 months out.) In our preparatory classes we had learned, in addition to navigation, military history, how to tie knots (I was shit at this bit), and proper officer conduct, that our main mission, the number one reason our military existed, was to discourage war. Most people, if they've heard of the concept, likely think of *nuclear* deterrence when it's referenced, though that's only part of the principle. Deterrence as a broad concept refers to the idea that our country's vast and capable armed services exist as a disincentive to war, not a solution in want of a problem. In theory, "bad guys" should look at our large navy, our massive army (and Marines, yes), and our high-tech air forces and, well, pee their pants. Do whatever they can to avoid provoking us. Obviously, on 9/11 the theory proved not applicable to non-state actors, but that's a different essay. The principle is valid nevertheless: our job was to get good at killing people so we'd never have to. So, you've got to wonder what the hell Trout was doing in all those classes. I mean, he graduated with better grades than I did, for sure, and yet he missed this thing, apparently, that had burrowed its way into *my* head, never to be extracted.

He was just one guy though, a minority opinion. As

for everybody else…Well, perhaps it's best to describe what I *didn't* see upon leaving my dorm that day. And what I *didn't* hear. Because their absence is what stands out in my memory more than anything.

Campus was eerie, a ghost town, if you'll pardon the cliché. Our sound effects friend has inserted whooshing wind into this segment to emphasize the desolation. I feared mentioning the quiet to my roommate, because then he'd have to chime in with "Yeah, a little too quiet," at which cue a bear might've burst out from behind a tree or something. Joking aside, it really is funny how the human brain lacks the ability to quantify some things before experiencing their dearth. For example, out here it should've been a constant drone of footsteps and chatter, some laughter tossed in, the occasional salutatory cheering. Instead….

Actually, more like……………………………………………..

I remember hearing the buses more than anything. They'd always been present as part of the background buzz, but that morning they roared running their normal routes, many devoid of passengers. Visually it was a similar story: lines of sight opened and I saw patches of grass, bushes, benches, trashcans I'd never spotted before, there being no packs of sorority girls or fraternity bozos blocking the view. In short, it didn't feel like a campus boasting 40,000+ students, at least not one on an early semester Tuesday morning. Hell, Sundays were often more crowded. Hot and humid as it was, I'll be damned if I didn't feel a chill traipsing through that wasteland.

Class, I know, was a bust, though I can't recall how

exactly that played out. Texas A&M University had an unwritten rule, probably found at other schools as well, stating class was dismissed if the professor didn't show up within fifteen minutes of start time, and I imagine this got invoked across campus. Or, perhaps my instructor showed up, found a scant crowd, and sent us home. Either way, the result was the same: I didn't have a real class that morning and was on my way back to the dorm far earlier than usual.

I found where everybody was, or at least a sampling. Taking a detour through a nearby "civilian" dorm complex to scope out the freshmen girls studying or buying pencils at the shop, I discovered the place packed with pajama-clad kids staring at the TVs scattered throughout. Some cried, some hugged each other, and I heard no shortage of sniffling. Remember, this was pre-smartphone, and it was rather *en vogue* for many first-semester students to forgo personal television ownership as a means to good grades, so assembling in such a manner was, for many, the only way to keep abreast of the situation. All good and well...but for the weeping and hugging, which didn't compute for me. In fact, it sent me scurrying.

At this point most folks would have thought it obvious classes were cancelled for the rest of the day, but not me. I tried to attend another that afternoon, Handball out at the Recreation Center. If I'd thought campus was dead before, I was in for a shock on that trek, even more of one upon arriving at the massive concrete-and-glass structure and finding it forsaken by all but the most committed muscle heads. Message received.

None of this had occurred to me, for which I blame a lifelong dependence on routine and an abiding fondness for following rules. I had a class scheduled for that morning and it was my duty, barring physical inability, to attend. Thus, the pit that had formed in my stomach as I'd briefly watched the tragedy unfold on television was not related to those images but to the prospect of being late to class. Having since been diagnosed with Obsessive-Compulsive Disorder, I can look back on this fixation and cut myself some slack, this being anxiety at work as opposed to soullessness.

Nothing's ever this simple, of course, but if there's more to the story, it means accepting that my subconscious may have been working on stuff my conscious mind didn't get a whiff of until later. The good thing about this theory is that it explains, somewhat, the churlishness I displayed throughout that day. Either that or I really am a cold-hearted bastard.

Accordingly, I propose that the idea of staying in my room to watch TV in shock did, in fact, cross my mind, only on a level below conscious awareness. And it got dismissed on that level before reaching the next, kind of like a slush-pile reader rejecting manuscripts so the editor doesn't have to. Though the OCD was largely responsible for that, a mean pragmatic streak lent a hand. Its rationale, so to speak, suggested staying in my dorm room was unlikely to help anyone experiencing the attacks. If you'd asked me at the time why I had attempted to go to class, I'd have said not doing so wouldn't have made a difference 1,500 miles away. Now, that, I'll admit, is cold, albeit entirely accurate. (It might help to know I am not, nor was I then, a religious man. Plus: Spock.)

Also accurate, if frigid in its logic: Every response I'd seen to the attacks, from Trout advocating war to students skipping class to collective mourning, might as well have been on some kind of terrorist wish list. Sure, they'd "succeeded" in killing thousands of people and demolishing a national symbol, but if such were their goals, wouldn't we just call them mass murders and vandals? We call them terrorists because they kill all those people and destroy stuff to induce terror, to provoke panic, to bring about change via emotional reaction. Think about it: every terrorist action, from the murders at the 1972 Munich Olympics, to the IRA bombings during The Troubles in the late 20th-century British Isles, to the attack on 9/11/2001, has a goal, which is hardly ever simply wanton carnage. Death and destruction are disruptors meant to instill fear and spur change, and it seemed to me the terrorists had at least accomplished the former and—spoiler alert—the U.S. is a vastly different country today than it was pre-9/11. I envisioned nameless, faceless terrorists celebrating as they watched news reports showing not just the ruination in Manhattan and the Pentagon but footage like what I'd witnessed: schools and businesses shut down, people crying and hugging each other, others waving flags.

Felt like we'd handed them a victory.

I never mentioned any of this until later, and only then in confidence and hushed tones, wearing a pained expression. For one thing, again, little of it was coherent at the time, especially the bit about the U.S. essentially forfeiting. But even before it became clear to me, I recognized how far afield I was from everyone else, how skewed was my attitude, how incongruent my reaction. The result of this self-censorship was an extended, if limited-scope bad attitude. Haughtiness, frustration, and irritation, lasting from the moment I saw the campus vacant until, jeez, if I said sometime in June of 2019, would you believe me? I was an emotionally stunted cretin, about as sophisticated as a mass-produced bathmat, and it showed. Constitutionally incapable of acknowledging any reaction but my own as potentially beneficial, I behaved like it. A therapist or teen TV show might call it "processing," but the truth is I couldn't understand some folks' need to watch history unfold. Instead, I dismissed it with derision. The communal grief I found perplexing and disorienting and thus beneath me. All this plus the day's general sense of disorder set me on edge, the anxiety manifesting as self-important surliness, for which I've suffered two decades of misplaced guilt.

Am I letting myself off the hook a bit here? Possibly. Spending time on the couch doesn't make me a psychologist, after all, so the preceding might've been so much bunk. And it is a fine line between rationalization and explanation. Nevertheless, while I still believe my analyses were valid, none of this is about saying I was right and everybody else was wrong. (Okay, maybe warmonger Trout was wrong. And the terrorists... duh.) It's about accepting my own humanity, warts and all.

Some might contend that using a national tragedy as a vehicle for such an emotional unburdening is crass. I disagree. (Obviously.) Recall Socrates's famous dictum: "The unexamined life is not worth living." Considering he supposedly said this during the trial that resulted in his death sentence, I think he's saying we're not limited to probing our existence through the everyday lens. In fact, I'd wager he'd encourage this particular endeavor precisely *because* it was so uncomfortable.

Anyway, if there's one thing definitely *not* on the terrorist wish list, it's psychological growth. And twenty years late is better than never.

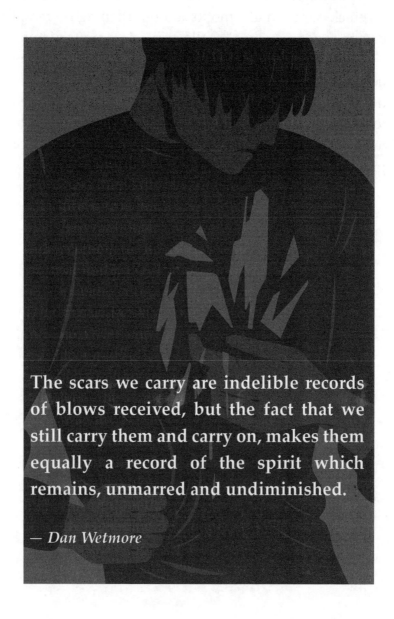

The scars we carry are indelible records of blows received, but the fact that we still carry them and carry on, makes them equally a record of the spirit which remains, unmarred and undiminished.

— *Dan Wetmore*

Shock and After-Shocks

Dan Wetmore

Sept. 11, 2001

It's just another bleary Tuesday morning at Vandenberg Air Force Base, jockeying with the clock to get out the door, when the phone rings.

At the other end, my wife's mother—two time zones east. Strange that she's calling at 7 a.m.

Doubly so that she wants her daughter to put her son-in-law on the line.

At a loss for anything else, I ask how she's doing. "The question..." she asks, "...is how are you?"

With her suggestion, I turn on the TV to find *Blues Clues* banished this morning. And if the sun wasn't just rising, I'd enjoy the impressive realism of the made-for-tv docudrama unfolding before me, safe behind the protective barrier of make-believe that most television in our house is.

Instead, standing in uniform in quarters where a long ago major viewed the Tet Offensive, an unknown lieutenant first saw men walk on the moon, and a different captain watched a wall being torn down, it's my turn to witness history pouring out.

The scene is surreal, made more so by the clair-voyeristic aspect of watching events still two hours in my West Coast future, already an hour in New York City's past.

Later, at work, I'm immobilized by unfocus, while activity goes on all around. I marvel at others' outward sameness, wondering if that is the best reaction, or absence of one. I fight feelings of helplessness — a gnawing frustration that, right now, given our removal from today's violence, the two might be one and the same.

Self-conscious about my immobility, I move to match others' motions. But I still feel outside it all, a spectator to some contest being played out according to rules I don't understand.

Sept. 14, 2001

Four days later, Friday, I head to the Officer's Club. I need to be surrounded by others who clump around in combat boots on a daily basis. I'm still not sure what I'm feeling, so lack words to express it. When that happens, we go to family, for whom words aren't needed and from whom none are demanded. There, in the press of people I'm regarding as an embrace, I sit at a far table. The corner TV feeds our regained focus on the world's growing pains. I hope they really are nothing more than the pains of growing up.

Oct. 18, 2001

Near the front gate, the flags formed up in a circle around the Minuteman III ICBM on static display are still hanging at half-mast. It angers me. They're like men bowed, looking to their feet; like the trees of the season, half undressed as they lose their leaves to don the raiment of the season of death.

I don't like it. I'm ready to start moving through and beyond, to something else.

June 14, 2002

Again, flags are everywhere. And not just because it's the second Friday in June and I'm standing high on a hillside, looking down on six acres of uncommonly uniform rows of red, white, and blue larkspurs, here in the fertile valley of Lompoc, California—flower seed capital of the world.

Any other year, this particular display might feel unique to this place. Usually the trappings of an observance fall off as you move farther from its center, like waves tend to diminish as they propagate outward.

But not this time.

If I had the eyes for it, I'm sure on this year's day I could spy that same density of ruby, diamond, and sapphire marching up H Street, across Buellton, along the spine of the Rockies, through Kansas, over the Alleghenies, to horizon's arc at the Atlantic.

Aug. 19, 2002

Waking to clocks blinking nonsense numbers in the pre-dawn, I'm aware of how otherwise dark it is everywhere—power outage.

I go to the window. Not to confirm, but to see if there might be men bent on harm running furtively down Korina Avenue.

It's too soon from sleep to be a conscious thought, just reflex. And waking enough to realize that, and knowing how reflexes are built, I see the shockwaves of eleven months remove are still rippling, strangely undamped by time.

Those waves, like the dreams I just left, linger below the surface—a constant, unconscious stimulus that moves me in ways I can't always anticipate.

Sometimes it's for the good—when I hold my six-year-old's gaze for extra seconds, striving to see beyond sight more palpably, and succeed in magnifying the moment large enough to be lived in. Or, when fumbling through the kindnesses strangers make to those who've suffered loss. Or watching an irritation, a friction, dissolve into nothing, sharing a knowing glance with another who saw it too, one that says, "This isn't really important."

Sometimes for the bad—snapping at shadows that are only shadows. Or seeing solicitation where there was only an expression of concern; or drawing back into a private pity, using my arms only to hold myself, instead of another who could use them more.

Aug. 25, 2002

So, we carry scars. Yet, we work at our physical therapies, struggling to reclaim/maintain the freedom of motion we knew before, perhaps even gain some new strength and flexibility.

We hope time both diminishes the pain and sustains the passion.

The scars we carry are indelible records of blows received, but the fact that we still carry them and carry on, makes them equally a record of the spirit which remains, unmarred and undiminished.

Political leadership is needed to condemn all terrorism and fund programs that promote mutual respect among racial, ethnic, religious, and gender groups throughout the U.S. ...and the world.

—*Dianne R. Layden*

Three Reflections

Dianne R. Layden

"The past is never dead. It's not even past."

William Faulkner, *Requiem for a Nun*, 1951
Nobel Prize for Literature, 1949

I live in the past, actually. I remember well September 11, 2001, as do many Americans. My three reflections are about what I saw and did that day and what I've learned since then about the 9/11 attacks and about terrorism.

1. What I Saw and Did

I lived in Santa Fe, New Mexico, and was getting ready to go to work when I saw a replay of the first airplane hitting the Twin Towers of the World Trade Center in New York City on ABC's "Good Morning America." At 6:46 a.m. Mountain Time (8:46 a.m. Eastern Time), American Airlines Flight 11 crashed into the upper floors of the North Tower. The news team assumed this was an accident, but the Twin Towers are 110 stories tall, and the team wondered how such an accident could happen on a clear, sunny day.

Then, at 7:03 a.m. Mountain Time, United Airlines Flight 175 crashed into the upper floors of the South Tower, and the news team knew it wasn't an accident.

Soon I saw the South Tower and then the North Tower fall. I cried, as I did when I saw the truck-bombed Alfred P. Murrah federal building, killing 168 people, in Oklahoma City in April 1995, and when I learned President John Kennedy was assassinated in Dallas in November 1963. I love America, mostly. My birthday is the Fourth of July and my academic field is American Studies.

In September 2001, I was Division Head of Business and Professional Studies at Santa Fe Community College. I went to work but couldn't concentrate while sitting in my office. The college showed national news on its big TV screen in the cafeteria, and I sat there and watched off and on all day.

I learned of the other two planes in the coordinated attack. American Airlines Flight 77 crashed into the Pentagon in Arlington, Virginia. United Airlines Flight 93 was hijacked on its way to San Francisco, but passengers learned of the Twin Towers attacks from air phone and cell phone calls, took over the plane from the hijackers, and crashed it into a field near Shanksville, Pennsylvania, so it wouldn't hit the Capitol Building or White House in Washington, D. C. To this day, the intended target of United 93 is unknown.

When such attacks occur, there may be a long wait for accurate information. At the time, I had studied violence for thirteen years and remembered the February 1993 truck bombing at the World Trade Center (WTC), a terrorist attack at the underground parking garage of the South Tower. Six people died.

2. *What Happened on 9/11*

My interest in 9/11 has continued since that day. In my college English classes, I've taught an essay about 9/11, "The First Hours" by Tim Townsend.[1] Published in October 2001 in a 9/11 special issue of *Rolling Stone Magazine*. Townsend's essay employs rich images in his account of when, as a *Wall Street Journal* finance reporter, he found himself five blocks from the WTC when the planes hit the Twin Towers. I felt as if I were walking beside him that morning.

He saw falling luggage, shoes, and body parts. When the plane hit the South Tower, Townsend wrote, the huge structure "seemed to suck the plane into itself. For an instant it looked like there would be no trauma to the building–it was as if the plane just slipped through a mail slot in the side of the tower, or simply vanished." Then came the fireball that "ballooned out of the top of the building."

Townsend also saw beauty. Jumpers from the North Tower fell with suit jackets "fluttering in the wind" and dresses "billowing like failed parachutes." At Battery Park, the ash that fell "on the grass and trees gave the park the peaceful feel of a light evening snowfall."

Ashamed, he confessed that, thinking he was running for his life, he ran past an older man who had fallen hard on the ground, his glasses knocked off. Townsend wrote he did not live up to his professed creed to "help the helpless." Others picked the man up and they all kept running.

Witnessing 9/11 affected Townsend. He ended his essay by telling readers that the next day, after drinking eight or nine beers, he cried and cried over what a nice gesture it was for the National Football League to consider postponing its second week of games. Townsend soon left New York City for a post as religion reporter for the *St. Louis Post-Dispatch*.

I've seen TV programs about various aspects of 9/11—firefighters who died or were injured in New York City and details of the crashes in Pennsylvania and at the Pentagon.

I have also seen several enlightening films about the personal stories of 9/11: *United 93*, *9/11: The Falling Man*, and *The Walk*.

United 93 reenacts the story of the plane that crashed in rural Pennsylvania; made without well-known actors, the acclaimed film focuses on the hijackers and passengers. Because the plane departed over forty minutes late, the passengers learned of the WTC attacks through phone calls. Many of the passengers and crew executed an assault on the hijackers, crashing the plane to the ground at 563 miles per hour and killing all forty-four aboard.[2] Just before they took action, passenger Todd Beamer was heard saying, "Are you guys ready? Let's roll!" The latter phrase soon was heard in songs and praise from President George W. Bush.[3] Lauded as heroes, they posthumously were awarded the Congressional Gold Medal.

The documentary film *9/11: The Falling Man* is about the attempt to identify a man, presumably a waiter at a top-floor World Trade Center (WTC) restaurant, who was photographed in his white jacket falling nearly straight down from one of the towers.[4] He is a reminder of the estimated 200 jumpers from the WTC after the planes hit the upper floors.

The Walk is a film that displays the Twin Towers decades before 9/11, when they were the tallest buildings in the world and far from disaster. In August 1974, with the help of a friend, Philippe Petit, the French high-wire walker, strung a 138-foot wire across the gap between the towers and, more than 1,300 feet above the ground, walked the wire for forty-five minutes without falling.

The loss of life, injuries to life, and dollar costs of 9/11 show the long reach of terrorism.

According to the 9/11 Memorial & Museum, between 16,400 and 18,000 people were in the WTC complex when the planes struck the Twin Towers; the vast majority evacuated safely.[5] 2,996 lives were lost immediately, including nineteen hijackers—2,606 at the WTC and surrounding area, including 343 firefighters and seventy-one law enforcement; 265 on the four airplanes; and 125 at the Pentagon, including fifty-five military.[6] Over 6,000 people were injured. By September 2018, an additional 156 police officers and 182 firefighters died, and 20,874 claimants were eligible for the 9/11 Compensation Fund, including 16,559 first responders.[7]

By contrast, in perhaps the only modern comparable attack on the U.S., 2,403 Americans and fifty-five Japanese died, and 1,178 Americans were wounded, when Japan bombed the U.S. naval base at Pearl Harbor,

Hawaii, on December 7, 1941.[8]

———∽◦∾———

In September 2011, the *New York Times* estimated the cost of 9/11 as $3.3 trillion to compensate for the human toll, including loss of life, injury and first responder medical care, and to replace destroyed and damaged property; for the economic impact, such as business interruption and reduced airline travel; for homeland security; for war funding in Iraq and Afghanistan following 9/11, including veteran medical care; and for future war funding in 2012-2016, including veteran medical care for forty years.[9] In November 2018, the Costs of War project at Brown University estimated total costs of $5.9 trillion to fund the war on terror and veteran medical care through Fiscal Year 2019.[10]

The United States knew Osama bin Laden directed the 9/11 attacks, which were planned for two years and carried out by nineteen Middle Eastern men, some of them at least partially trained as pilots in Florida. Bin Laden explained his motivation in a November 2004 videotape he sent to the news channel AlJazeera.com: "…[W]e should punish the oppressor in kind and…we should destroy towers in America in order that they taste some of what we tasted and so that they be deterred from killing our women and children."[11] "In kind" refers to American involvement in the Israeli invasion of Lebanon, starting in 1982, which bin Laden described as "rockets raining down on our home without mercy." He averred many were killed, injured, terrorized, and displaced, and their housing was destroyed.

I didn't cry when I learned bin Laden was killed by American agents in May 2011.

3. Aftermath: Rise of Domestic Terrorism in the U.S.

For me, the aftermath of 9/11 is related to my thirty years of research on violence: hate crimes, workplace and campus violence, public violence, terrorism, and mass shootings. After 9/11, I began reading about terrorism, both foreign and domestic. Because of the recent rise in the domestic variety, 9/11 has never ended for me—like the film *Groundhog Day*, in which the main character keeps reliving the same day. Every so many days, another terrorist act is committed or thwarted somewhere in the U.S.

Under federal law, "international terrorism," such as 9/11, refers to violent actions or "acts dangerous to human life" that violate U.S. or state criminal laws; intend to intimidate or coerce a civilian population, influence government policy by intimidation or coercion, or affect government conduct by mass destruction, assassination, or kidnapping; and occur outside the U.S. or "transcend national boundaries in terms of the means by which they are accomplished, the persons they appear intended to intimidate or coerce, or the locale in which their perpetrators operate or seek asylum..."[12] "Domestic terrorism" refers to acts dangerous to human life that occur primarily within U.S. territorial jurisdiction.

Since 9/11, terrorism reports indicate no foreign terrorist group has conducted a deadly attack successfully in the U.S. But, following actions by the Islamic State of Iraq and Syria (ISIS), Americans have engaged in numerous domestic terrorist attacks.[13] The most glaring threat to the U.S. today is domestic terrorism.[14]

Examples of domestic terrorism since 2013 include the Boston Marathon bombings, U.S. mail bombing attempts, and mass shootings such as occurred at an Oak Creek, Wisconsin, Sikh church in 2012; a Charleston, South Carolina, African-American church; a Colorado Springs, Colorado, Planned Parenthood office; a county employee Christmas party in San Bernardino, California; a Congressional baseball game in Alexandria, Virginia; a Pittsburgh, Pennsylvania, synagogue, and an El Paso, Texas, Walmart.

Evidence indicates the San Bernardino mass shooting was inspired by ISIS. Motivations for mass shootings range from international political rivalry to racial, ethnic, and religious hatred to personal disputes to undetermined motives, as in the case of Stephen Paddock, who killed 58 people in 2017 at a music festival in Las Vegas, Nevada. The Oak Creek, Charleston, Pittsburgh, and El Paso mass shootings were hate crimes. Abortion providers such as Planned Parenthood have endured violence since the 1970s, including vandalism, assault, bombing, arson, kidnapping, and murder. Fortunately, numerous potential acts of domestic terrorism have been thwarted by federal, state, and local law enforcement, and some of these acts were inspired by ISIS.[15]

An FBI report provides a list of terrorist acts in 1980-2005, with descriptions of terrorist acts in 2002-2005.[16] A publicly available terrorism database is lacking, however, to provide a full picture. In May 2019, FBI testimony before Congress identified about 850 domestic terrorism investigations were being pursued across the country.[17] H.R. 3106, the Domestic and International Terrorism DATA Act, introduced in June 2019, would provide information about the number of terrorism-related investigations, indictments, prosecutions, and convictions.[18] The bill was passed by the House of Representatives and forwarded to the Senate in October 2019.[19]

The rise of domestic terrorism since 9/11 is now addressed in *Strategic Framework for Countering Terrorism and Targeted Violence*, issued by the U.S. Department of Homeland Security in September 2019. In recent years, the report states, domestic terrorists have caused more deaths than foreign terrorists; domestic terrorist attacks and hate crime attacks sometimes overlap; white supremacist violent extremism is a potent force driving domestic terrorism; and although lone individuals generally commit these attacks, they are part of a broader movement, which often combine prejudices against groups.[20] Through technology, white supremacist violent extremists are increasingly transnational in outlook, similar to how ISIS inspired and connected with potential radical Islamist terrorists across the world. Thus, one long-term consequence of 9/11 is international terrorism may have increased domestic terrorism in the U.S.

Conclusion

For me, 9/11 is unforgettable. I continue to read about it and understand the need for health care funding for 9/11 responders.[21] Political leadership is needed to condemn all terrorism and fund programs that promote mutual respect among racial, ethnic, religious, and gender groups throughout the U.S. ...and the world.

Footnotes

1 - Tim Townsend. "The First Hours." *Rolling Stone Magazine*, Issue 880, October 25, 2001, pp. 46-47. See also Michael Kimmel. "Gender, Class, and Terrorism." *Chronicle of Higher Education*. *Chronicle.com*, February 8, 2002, www.oswego.edu/~mccune/wst200_eadingmasc. Accessed April 13, 2019. Kimmel found commonalities among Mohamed Atta, leader of the 9/11 attacks; Adolf Hitler, Nazi German dictator in World War II; and Timothy McVeigh, Oklahoma City bomber. I also teach this essay in English classes.

2 - "United Airlines Flight 93." *Wikipedia.org*, May 24, 2019, http://govinfo.library.unt.edu/ 911/report/911Report_Ch1.htm. Accessed June 6, 2019. See also "Chapter 1: We Have Some Planes." National Commission on Terrorist Attacks upon the United States. 9/11 Commission Report. *9-11Commision.gov*, 2004, https://www.9-11commission.gov/ report/911Report.pdf. Accessed June 6, 2019.

3 - Jada Yuan. "Let's Roll." *New York Magazine*, August 27, 2011, http://nymag.com/news/ 9-11/10th-anniversary/lets-roll/. Accessed June 6, 2019.

4 - *TIME Magazine*. "9/11: The Falling Man, Behind the Photo." *YouTube.com*, September 8, 2016, www.youtube.com/watch?v= SMDkv-JRHaNM. Accessed April 11, 2019. See also Tom Junod. "The Falling Man: An Unforgettable Story." *Esquire.com*, September 9, 2016, www.esquire.com/news-politics/a48031/ the-falling-man-tom-junod/. Accessed April 11, 2019.

5 - 9/11 Memorial & Museum. "FAQ about 9/11: What happened at the World Trade Center on 9/11?" *911Memorial.org*, n.d., www.911memorial.org/faq-about-911. Accessed April 9, 2019.

6 - "Casualties of the September 11 Attacks." *Wikipedia.org*, April 10, 2019, en.wikipedia.org/wiki/Casualties_of_the_September_11_attacks. Accessed April 11, 2019.

7 - Aaron Katersy. "The 9/11 toll still grows: More than 16,000 Ground Zero responders who got sick found eligible for awards." *ABCNews.com*, September 10, 2018, abcnews.go.com/ US/911-toll-growsl-16000-ground-responders-sick-found/story?id=57669657. Accessed April 12, 2019.

8 - "Remembering Pearl Harbor: A Pearl Harbor Fact Sheet." The National WWII Museum. *Census.gov*, n.d., https://www.census.gov/history/pdf/pearl-harbor-fact-sheet-1.pdf. Accessed June 11, 2019.

9 - Shan Carter and Amanda Cox. "One 9/11 Tally: $3.3 Trillion." *NewYorkTimes.com*, September 8, 2011, archive.nytimes.com/www.ny-times.com/interactive/2011/09/08/us/sept-11-reckoning/cost-graphic.html?hp. Accessed April 11, 2019.

10 - Neta C. Crawford. "United States Budgetary Costs of the Post-9/11 Wars Through FY2019: $5.9 Trillion Spent and Obligated." *Watson.Brown.edu*, November 14, 2018, watson.brown.edu/research/2018/59-trillion-spent-and-obligated-post-911-wars. Accessed April 12, 2019.

11 - "Full Transcript of bin Laden's Speech." *AlJazeera.com*, November 1, 2004, www.aljazeera.com/archive/2004/11/%20200849163336457223.html?xif=)%20I%20so% 20wish%20he%20would%20have%20chosen%20cooperation%20and%20compromis. Accessed April 10, 2019.

12 - Legal Information Institute. "18 U.S. Code, Section 2331. Definitions." *Law.Cornell.edu*, n.d., www.law.cornell.edu/uscode/text/18/2331. Accessed April 14, 2019.

13 - Jihadist Terrorism 17 Years After 9/11: What is the Threat to the United States?" *NewAmerica.org*, n.d., https://www.newamerica.org/international-security/reports/jihadist-terrorism-17-years-after-911/what-is-the-threat-to-the-united-states/. Accessed June 10, 2019.

14 - Peter Bergen and David Sterman. "The Real Terrorist Threat in America: It's No Longer Jihadist Groups." *ForeignAffairs.com*, October 30, 2018, https:// www.foreignaffairs.com/articles/united-states/2018-10-30/real-terrorist-threat-america. Accessed June 10, 2019.

15 - Linh Bui, Justin Juvenal, and Dan Morse. "After admiring Islamic State fighters, Maryland man decided to emulate them, prosecutors assert." *WashingtonPost.com*, April 9, 2019, www.washingtonpost.com/local/ public-safety/man-accused-of-plotting-isis-inspired-attack-at-dulles-airport-and-national-harbor-to-appear-in-court/2019/04/09/55d49444-5abc-11e9-842d-7d3ed7eb3957_story.html?. Accessed April 15, 2019.

16 - U.S. Department of Justice. Federal Bureau of Investigation. *Terrorism: 2002-2005. FBI.gov*, n.d., https:// www.fbi.gov/file-repository/ stats-services-publications-terrorism-2002-2005-terror02_05.pdf/   view. Accessed October 26, 2019.

17 - Greg Myre. "FBI Is Investigating 850 Cases of Potential Domestic Terrorism." *NPR.org*, May 8, 2019, https://www.npr. org/2019/05/08/721552539/fbi-is-investigating-850-cases-of-potential-domestic-terrorism. Accessed October 26, 2019.

18 - U.S. Rep. Bennie G. Thompson (D-Miss.). "We need the full picture of domestic terrorism." *TheHill.com*, September 17, 2019, https:// thehill.com/blogs/congress-blog/homeland-security/461650-we-need-the-full-picture-on-domestic-terrorism. Accessed October 26, 2019. See also Devlin Barrett. "Arrests in domestic terror probes outpace those inspired by Islamic terrorists. *WashingtonPost.com*, March 8, 2019, https:// www.washingtonpost.com/world/national-security/arrests-in-domestic-terror-probes-outpace-those-inspired-by-islamic-extremists/ 2019/03/08/0bf329b6-392f-11e9-a2cd-307b06d0257b_story.html. Accessed October 26, 2019.

19 - H.R. 3106 – Domestic and International Terrorism DATA Act. 116th Congress (2019-2020). Referred to the Senate on October 15, 2019, *Congress. gov*, https://www.congress.gov/ bill/116th-congress/house-bill/3106/text. Accessed October 26, 3019.

20 - U.S. Department of Homeland Security. "Strategic Framework for Countering Terrorism and Targeted Violence." *DHS.gov*, September 2019, https://www.dhs.gov/sites/ default/files/publications/19_0920_plcy_strategic-framework-countering-terrorism-targeted-violence.pdf, p. 10. Accessed October 13, 2019.

21 - CNN Library. "September 11 Victim Aid and Compensation Fact Facts." *CNN.com*, September 2, 2019, https://www.cnn.com/2013/07/27/us/september-11th-victim-aid-and-compensation-fast-facts/index.html. Accessed October 21, 2019.

After 9/11, everything everywhere was different. People were nicer, more patient and kind.

— Marilyn L. Pettes Hill

Three thousand lives
torn from our hands,
but where they lie
our memory stands.

—Dan Wetmore

Crucible

Dan Wetmore

The Stars & Stripes
as somber shroud
we view through tears
which vision clouds.
Three thousand lives
torn from our hands,
but where they lie
our memory stands.
And builds resolve
where towers once grew,
with hopes to make
the world anew;
to see all neighbors
in a mirror –
hate only Hate,
our vision clearer.
That those who died...
not mourned in vain,
lifting us, in their wake,
'bove mortal plane.

New Mexico will never forget 9/11.

Author Biographies

JOE BROWN

Joe Brown is pursuing a long-time passion, writing a memoir and fiction while supporting music. He served on the New Mexico State Music Commission and the International Board of Directors of the Western Music Association. Mr. Brown retired from military and civil service careers in 2010 as Senior Analyst advising the Commander, Air Force Flight Test Center. He advised on strategic issues collaborating with senior national planners across the Department of Defense Test and Evaluation Enterprise.

Veterans Portrait Project by Stacy Pearsall

JOHN J. CANDELARIA

John J. Candelaria is a narrative poet who enjoys writing poetry in form and free verse. He has authored a poetry book titled, *War in the Company of Medics: Poems of the 45th Surgical Hospital in Vietnam.* His poems have been published in Southwest Writer's *Storyteller Anthology,* the *OASIS Journal,* SouthWest Writers's *Sage,* as well as by the Haiku Society of America and the Tanka Society of America.

Photo by Rose Marie Kern

PETE CHRISTENSEN

Pete Christensen is an actor and author who's written two books and two novels. He's also a newspaper columnist, and blogger. He's hosted TV programs in Milwaukee WI, and Flagstaff, AZ, and is an award-winning radio broadcaster.

Photo by Marci Frederick

TERESA CIVELLO

Terry was an eye witness to the World Trade Center attack and watched from her street corner as each tower became a fireball within twenty minutes. An award-winning author of memoir short stories, Terry has never returned to the site where for years she had attended government meetings as a city-agency representative and later as a consultant.

Photo by Nancy Vigil, Angeleyes Photography

BRENDA COLE

Brenda Cole grew up along the Mississippi River in Eastern Iowa and became a New Mexican over twenty-three years ago. Devouring the written word has always been a passion of hers. Writing them began in earnest at age thirteen, winning her first contest with a science fiction short story. Brenda has written and edited works in life sciences, archaeology, poetry, and fiction. Her current interest is writing short stories and memoir.

Photo by Kate the Photographer

SYLVIA RAMOS CRUZ

Sylvia Ramos Cruz writes poems inspired by works of art, women's lives, and every-day injustices. Her award-winning poetic essays, poems, and photographs have appeared in both local and national publications. *Railyards Trilogy: Poems and Photographs,* multimedia collage work, is in the City of Albuquerque's Public Art collection. Currently, she is researching and writing the history of woman suffrage in New Mexico. She is a retired surgeon, world traveler, avid gardener, and fully-engaged women's rights activist.

Photo by Jesse Ehrenberg

MARY E. DORSEY

Mary E. Dorsey is 70+/ retired RN/2X AML-Leukemia survivor. She loves animals—especially cats. She walks each morning and has been writing since childhood. Mary writes all types of material including poetry, stories, novels in any form, style, or on any subject. She is a member of Southwest Writers and the New Mexico Poetry Society. Mary lives in Albuquerque, NM with her beloved fur babies: "domesticated," neutered feral, and stray. She's honored that *September* was chosen for this book.

Photo by Virginia Lucero

JESSE EHRENBERG

Jesse Ehrenberg moved to New Mexico from New York in the early 1970s. He started writing poetry as a teenager and has never seen any reason to stop. In 2018 his book, *SURPRISE!*, won prizes for both cover and content from New Mexico Press Women, and in 2019 it won a Silver Award in the inaugural Margaret Randall Poetry Book Contest. His work can also be found in many New Mexico poetry anthologies.

Photo by Sylvia Ramos Cruz

COLIN PATRICK ENNEN

Colin Patrick Ennen lives in Albuquerque where he works at a doggie daycare and has one of his own dogs, named Shylock. He counts among his literary heroes Edgar Allan Poe, Kurt Vonnegut, the dude who wrote *Beowulf,* and, of course, Shakespeare. His stories have appeared in two volumes from B-Cubed Press (*More Alternative Truths* and *Alternative Theologies*), on the website *Writers Resist,* and in the 2018 *Sage Anthology* from Southwest Writers. Find him on Twitter @cpennen.

Photo by Noelani Daniel

ROGER FLOYD

Roger Floyd received his Ph.D. degree in virology in 1971, and has worked for Baylor College of Medicine, Methodist Hospital Houston, Duke University, The University of North Carolina, and The University of Cincinnati, where he performed virology research and clinical virology. In retirement in Albuquerque, NM, he writes science fiction novels, literary short stories, and a small amount of poetry. He's written three science fiction novels which are in various stages of preparation for publication.

Photo by John Husler

RYAN P. FREEMAN

Born in Portland, Oregon, Ryan's been devouring books ever since he learned to read. He loves the smell of rain, the rumble of storms, and the scent of pine forests. Since he began publishing fantasy works in 2016, Ryan has also become an active member of the St. Louis Writers Guild, and founded the Hannibal Writers Guild. He is represented by Patty Carothers of Metamorphosis Literary Agency.

Photo courtesy Ryan P. Freeman

CORNELIA GAMLEM

Cornelia Gamlem is an author, consultant, and speaker. She's co-authored four books: *The Big Book of HR, The Essential Workplace Conflict Handbook, The Conflict Resolution Phrase Book, and The Manager's Answer Book* and co-writes a weekly blog, *Making People Matter*. A nationally recognized HR expert, she's testified before the EEOC, been quoted in major publications such as the *New York Times*, and contributed articles to publications including *Fast Company* and *Forbes*.

Photo by Derek Winfield

PAUL D. GONZALES

A native-born son from Pittsburgh, Pennsylvania, two weeks after graduation from High School in 1966, Paul D. Gonzales joined the U.S. Army. He pursued a career in Radiology as a Radiographic Imaging Specialist and spent forty-six years in his chosen profession. Paul believes words have power that allow him to have a voice on subjects that matter to his "inner man."

Photo by Ysela Gonzales

LORETTA HALL

Loretta Hall is a freelance writer and nonfiction book author. She has written eight books, including two on architecture and four on the history and future of space travel. She is a board member of New Mexico Press Women, a Space Ambassador for the National Space Society, and a member of the Historical Society of New Mexico's Speakers Bureau. In 2016, she was named Communicator of Achievement by the National Federation of Press Women.

Photo by Lifetouch

JOYCE HERTZOFF

Joyce Hertzoff retired in 2008 after forty-five years in the scientific literature publishing business. Since then, she's published three novels in the science fantasy *Crystal Odyssey* series, the novella *A Bite of the Apple*. She won first place in the 2017 NMPW contest in the YA fiction category, and *So You Want to be a Dragon*, a middle-grade book. Four short stories were included in anthologies. Joyce is a mentor and facilitator at Writers Village University and a member of Southwest Writers.

Photo by Ira Hertzoff

MARILYN L. PETTES HILL

Marilyn L. Pettes Hill was born in New Mexico. She received a Master's in Public Administration from New Mexico State University and had a successful career in government. She is vice president of a family business and she is married, has two sons and three delightful granddaughters. Marilyn loves to read, write, travel and spent time with family and friends.

Photo by Kim Jew

ROSE MARIE KERN

Rose Marie Kern began her career in Air Traffic Control (ATC) in 1983. During her thirty-four-year career she won three national awards for her work with the pilot community. She's written over 1,000 articles about ATC for pilot publications and has two books currently available: *Air to Ground 2020* which is a Guide for Pilots to the world of Air Traffic Control, and her memoir, *Stress is Relative*.

Photo Courtesy of Rose Marie Kern

CAROLYN KUEHN

Carolyn Kuehn has been a writer, editor, and marketing consultant for over twenty years. She is the author of the children's book *Victor's Garden* (Scholastic, 2013) and contributor to multiple magazines and newspapers, including *Voices in Urban Education, New Mexico Kids!, Family* magazine, *The Sun, The Philadelphia Inquirer,* and others. After twenty years in Philadelphia, Carolyn moved to Albuquerque, New Mexico, where she lives with her husband, two children, and two rescue dogs.

Photo by Russell Maynor

GAYLE LAURADUNN

Gayle Lauradunn's *Reaching for Air* is a Finalist for Best First Book of Poetry (Texas Institute of Letters). *All the Wild and Holy: A Life of Eunice Williams, 1696-1785* received Honorable Mention for the May Sarton Poetry Prize. Her poems have appeared in *Lumox 7*, *Earth* anthology, *Fixed and Free*, *Adobe Walls*, and many other journals. She served on the committee that selected Albuquerque's first Poet Laureate.

Photo by Patricia Walkow

DIANNE R. LAYDEN

Dianne R. Layden, Ph.D. is a semi-retired college professor and an award-winning writer. She came to Albuquerque in 1969 to pursue a doctorate in American Studies at the University of New Mexico. Dr. Layden held faculty posts at the University of Houston-Clear Lake and University of Redlands in Southern California, as well as in New Mexico. She has studied violence for over thirty years and New Mexico history and culture for over ten years.

Photo by Kate the Photographer

ELAINE CARSON MONTAGUE

Elaine Carson Montague is an author-educator who believes diverse needs require diverse solutions, which she loves to craft. In 2019, Elaine co-authored her first book, award-winning *Victory from the Shadows*, with her husband, Gary Ted Montague, to recount his growing up in a school for the blind and beyond and to help others with low vision. She writes from the heart and loves God, music, mountains, sunsets, and New Mexico chile.

Photo by LifeTouch Photography

JANET RUTH

Janet Ruth is a retired New Mexico ornithologist. Her writing focuses on connections to the natural world. She has poems in *Spiral Orb*, *Santa Fe Literary Review*, *Ekphrastic Review*, and in anthologies, including *Missing Persons: reflections on dementia*. Her book, *Feathered Dreams* (2018) was named Finalist for 2018 NM/AZ Book Awards. https://redstartsandravens.com/janets-poetry/

Photo by David Kruepe

PATRICIA WALKOW

Patricia Walkow is an author as well as curator and editor of this anthology. She is editor emeritus of *Corrales MainStreet News.* Her editing has been honored by New Mexico Press Women and the National Federation of Press Women. Her writing has won awards at the state, national, and international levels for full-length books, short stories, and essays. She contributes regularly to newspapers, magazines, and anthologies and is a founding member of The Corrales Writing Group and on the Board of Directors of SouthWest Writers.

Photo by Kate the Photographer

WALTER WALKOW

Walter Walkow works in the data sciences group at Sandia National Laboratories in New Mexico. He is an occasional contributor to publications of the Corrales Writing Group and has written articles for *Corrales MainStreet News.* As a child immigrant from post-World War II Germany, English syntax is sometimes challenging, but he has an editor-wife who helps him. Walter is an avid golfer and lives with his wife and pets in the village of Corrales, New Mexico.

Photo by Patricia Walkow

DAN WETMORE

Dan Wetmore is a military retiree who's attempting to turn a life-long avocation into a second vocation. Having landed far west of the Mississippi, he enjoys anchoring a chair at a local Starbucks under the pretense of writing, hikes in the high desert mountains, and wrenching on various old cars.

Photo courtesy of Dan Wetmore

Illustration and Photo Credits
in order of appearance

Map: boreala/Shutterstock.com
Attack sites: Patricia Walkow

Rudy Lopez Photography/
Shutterstock.com

Kristy Swanson/Shutterstock.com

Carlos Gandiaga/Shutterstock.com

Dan Howell/Shutterstock.com

Alexander Prokopenko/
Shutterstock.com

Frontpage/Shutterstock.com

Everett Historical/Shutterstock.com

Joseph Sohm/Shutterstock.com

Steve Heap/Shutterstock.com

Steve Heap/Shutterstock.com

Steve Heap/Shutterstock.com

jokerpro/Shutterstock.com
Text: Roger Floyd

Moonflies Photo/Shutterstock.com
Text: Marilyn L. Pettes Hill

siam.pukkato/Shutterstock.com
Text: Brenda Cole

NiP STUDIO/Shutterstock.com
Text: Elaine Carson Montague

Tinxi/Shutterstock.com
Text: Carolyn Kuehn

melitas/Shutterstock.com
Text: Brenda Cole

Crying Wolf/Shutterstock.com
Text: John J. Candelaria

pixfly/Shutterstock.com

Eugene Berman/Shutterstock.com
Text: Joe Brown

Image: Makhnach_S/Shutterstock.com
Text: Rose Marie Kern

Ron Dale/Shutterstock.com
Text: Pete Christensen

Alrandir/Shutterstock.com
Text: Janet Ruth

igor kisselev/Shutterstock.com

Lidiia/Shutterstock.com
Text: Ryan P. Freeman

Elena Rudyk/Shutterstock.com
Text: Mary E. Dorsey

DestroLove/Shutterstock.com
Text: Sylvia Ramos Cruz

paprika/Shutterstock.com
Text: Jesse Ehrenberg

sumikophoto/Shutterstock

Lightspring/Shutterstock.com
Text: Patricia Walkow and Walter Walkow

Anthony Correia/Shutterstock.com
Text: Joyce Hertzoff

David P. Smith/Shutterstock.com
Text: Cornelia Gamlem

Fabio Balbi/Shutterstock.com
Text: Loretta Hall

korkeng/Shutterstock.com
Text: Paul D. Gonzales

LEE SNIDER PHOTO IMAGES/Sutter-
stock.com
Text: Teresa Civello

Athapet Piruksa/Shutterstock.com
Text: Gayle Lauradunn

Tricia Daniel/Shutterstock.com
Text: Colin Patrick Ennen

GoodStudio/Shutterstock.com
Text: Dan Wetmore

Alexandria, Egypt 2006/
Patricia Walkow
Text: Dianne R. Layden

Vibrant Image Studio/Shutterstock.com
Text: Dan Wetmore

Sky image: jokerpro/Shutterstock.com
Never forget: Glynnis Jones/
Shutterstock.com
Composite: Patricia Walkow